T0362912

ABOUT THIS SERIES

....But after that, I realised that I knew very little about these parents of mine. They had been born about the start of the Twentieth Century, and they died in 1970 and 1980. For their last 20 years, I was old enough to speak with a bit of sense.

I could have talked to them a lot about their lives. I could have found out about the times they lived in. But I did not. I know almost nothing about them really. Their courtship? Working in the pits? The Lock-out in the Depression? Losing their second child? Being dusted as a miner? The shootings at Rothbury? My uncles killed in the War? Love on the dole? There were hundreds, thousands of questions that I would now like to ask them. But, alas, I can't. It's too late.

Thus, prompted by my guilt, I resolved to write these books. They describe happenings that affected people, real people. The whole series is, to coin a modern phrase, designed to push your buttons, to make you remember and wonder at things forgotten.

The books might just let nostalgia see the light of day, so that oldies and youngies will talk about the past and re-discover a heritage otherwise forgotten. Hopefully, they will spark discussions between generations, and foster the asking and answering of questions that should not remain unanswered.

BORN IN 1967?

WHAT ELSE HAPPENED?

RON WILLIAMS

AUSTRALIAN SOCIAL HISTORY

BOOK 29 IN A SERIES OF 35
FROM 1939 to 1973

War Babies Years (1939 to 1945):   7 Titles

Baby Boom Years (1946 to 1960):   15 Titles

Post Boom Years (1961 to 1970):   13 Titles

BOOM, BOOM BABY, BOOM

PUBLICATION DETAILS

BORN IN 1967? WHAT ELSE HAPPENED?
BOOM BOOKS

Web: www.boombooks.biz
Email: email@boombooks.biz

© Ron Williams 2013. This edition 2023

A single chapter or part thereof may be copied and reproduced without permission, provided that the Author, Title, ISBN and Web Site are acknowledged.

Creator: Williams, Ron, 1934- author
Title: Born in 1967? : what else happened? / Ron Williams.
Edition: Premier edition
Australia--History--Miscellanea--20th century.
ISBN: 9780995354968

Some Letters used in this text may still be in copyright. Every reasonable effort has been made to locate the writers. If any persons or their estates can establish authorship, and want to discuss copyright, please contact the author at email@boombooks.biz

Cover image: National Archives of Australia A1200, L49364, PM Harold Holt; A1200, L491571, Gough Whitlam MP; A12100, L51238, girl's fashions; A1200, L52406, school tuckshop; C4078, N22131, post office.

TABLE OF CONTENTS

BACKGROUND TO VIETNAM	3
DO WE LIKE ASIANS?	6
KIDS EVERYWHERE	15
A MAN IN CLERGY'S CLOTHING	23
SCOUTS AND GUIDES	29
LITTERBUGGERS	34
JUMPING HORSES	43
THE HORRORS OF RODEO	47
THE YANKS ARE COMING	55
BABY BONUS?	59
HOLT'S PARTY	74
CIVIL LIBERTIES AND VIETNAM	75
THOUGHTS ON PAPUA NEW GUINEA	83
THE YEAR OF THE POST-CODE	86
LAWS FOR HOMOSEXUALS	97
RIOTS IN THE USA	101
PARAPLEGICS	107
FROG-GATE	113
THE VALUE OF DRUNKS	119
BRISBANE IS STILL ASLEEP	124
TEENY BOPPERS STONED	133
WHY MIGRANTS LEAVE	136
SUMMING UP VIETNAM	149
SUMMING UP 1967	153

IMPORTANT PEOPLE AND EVENTS

Queen of England	Elizabeth II
Prime Minister of Oz	Harold Holt
Leader of Opposition	Arthur Calwell
Governor General	Lord Casey
The Pope	Paul VI
US President	Lyndon Johnson
PM of Britain (after April)	Harold Wilson

Holder of the Ashes:

1964	Australia 1 - 0
1965-66	Australia 1 - 1
1968	Australia 1 - 1

Melbourne Cup Winners:

1966	Galillee
1967	Red Handed
1968	Rain Lover

Academy Awards, 1967:

Best Actor	Paul Scofield
Best Actress	Elizabeth Taylor
Best Movie	A Man for all Seasons

PREFACE TO THIS SERIES

This book is the 29th in **a series** of books that I have researched and written. It tells a story about a number of important or newsworthy Australia-centric events that happened in 1967. The **series** covers each of the years from 1939 to 1973, for a total of 35 books.

I developed my interest in writing these books a few years ago at a time when my children entered their teens. My own teens started in 1947, and I tried to remember what had happened to me then. I thought of the big events first, like Saturday afternoon at the pictures, and cricket in the back yard, and the wonderful fun of going to Maitland on the train for school each day. Then I recalled some of the not-so-good things. I was an altar boy, and that meant three or four Masses a week. I might have thought I loved God at that stage, but I really hated his Masses. And the schoolboy bullies, like Greg Favel and the hapless Freddie Bevin. Yet, to compensate for these, there was always the beautiful, black headed, blue-sailor-suited June Brown, who I was allowed to worship from a distance.

I also thought about my parents. Most of the major events that I lived through came to mind readily. But after that, I realised that I really knew very little about these parents of mine. They had been born about the start of the Twentieth Century, and they died in 1970 and 1980. For their last 20 years, I was old enough to speak with a bit of sense. I could have talked to them a lot about their lives. I could have found out about the times they lived in. But I did not. I know almost nothing about them really. Their courtship? Working in the pits? The Lock-out in the Depression?

Losing their second child? Being dusted as a miner? The shootings at Rothbury? My uncles killed in the War? There were hundreds, thousands of questions that I would now like to ask them. But, alas, I can't. It's too late.

Thus, prompted by my guilt, I resolved to write these books. They describe happenings that affected people, real people. In **1967,** there is some coverage of international affairs, but a lot more on social events within Australia. This book, and the whole series is, to coin a modern phrase, designed to push the reader's buttons, to make you remember and wonder at things forgotten. The books might just let nostalgia see the light of day, so that oldies and youngies will talk about the past and re-discover a heritage otherwise forgotten. Hopefully, they will spark discussions between generations, and foster the asking and the answering of questions that should not remain unanswered.

The sources of my material. I was born in 1934, so that I can remember well a great deal of what went on around me from 1939 onwards. But of course, the bulk of this book's material came from research. That meant that I spent many hours in front of a computer reading electronic versions of newspapers, magazines, Hansard, Ministers' Press releases and the like. My task was to sift out, **day-by-day**, those stories and events that would be of interest to the most readers. Then I supplemented these with materials from books, broadcasts, memoirs, biographies, government reports and statistics. And I talked to old-timers, one-on-one, and in organised groups, and to Baby Boomers about their recollections. People with stories to tell came out of the woodwork, and talked no end about the tragic, and funny, and commonplace events that have shaped their lives.

The presentation of each book. For each year covered, the end result is a collection of short Chapters on many of the topics that concerned ordinary people in that year.

I think I have covered most of the major issues that people then were interested in. On the other hand, in some cases I have dwelt a little on minor frivolous matters, perhaps to the detriment of more sober considerations. Still, in the long run, this makes the book more readable, and hopefully it will convey adequately the spirit of the times.

Each of the books is mainly Sydney based, but I have been **deliberately national in outlook**, so that readers elsewhere will feel comfortable that I am talking about matters that affected them personally. After all, housing shortages and strikes and juvenile delinquency involved **all** Australians, and other issues, such as problems overseas, had no State component in them. Overall, I expect I can make you wonder, remember, rage and giggle equally, no matter whence you hail.

BACKGROUND TO 1967

I have written 35 books in this series so far. In the first seven of them, 1939 to 1945, I had a feeling of foreboding because I knew full well that they were the War years, and that impossibly difficult times were ahead.

From 1945, and right up till 1966, I had a happier message. Every year, I could say that things had improved on the previous year, and hopefully that they would be even better next year. In that latter hope, I was in general correct, for most of the population. For one thing, lots of servicemen came home, and were slowly, ever so slowly, taken out of their uniforms. Boys and girls got down to the serious business of courting, and marrying and starting a great baby boom.

Any able-bodied person could find a job, and could enter the great frustrating struggle to get accommodation away from their parents. Gradually, they **did** get their own houses, and cars, and second mortgages, and later TV sets, and of course, Hills Hoists in the backyard. Around them, the nation was doing well too, with only a few wobbles now and then. In the early 1950's, much of the nation actually boomed when the prices of wool and commodities reached record levels as a result of the Korean War.

For the majority of the population, the **pre-war image** was one of the ploughman homeward plodding his weary way. His dwelling was squalid, his wages were meagre, his wife spent her Mondays sweating over the washing, and her Tuesdays over the ironing. The kids were often bare-footed, poorly nourished, and beset with tooth aches, measles, and mumps. Most of them lived in handed-down clothes, and were a blanket short in winter.

From 1945, this melancholy picture had steadily and quickly changed. By the start of 1967, things were entirely different and all the deficiencies that I described above were scarcely on the agenda. For example, new three-bedroom homes in good suburbs were common, some people were getting second cars, schools were adequate, and the price of clothing had fallen beyond anyone's wildest dreams. What I am saying is that materially, every able-bodied person was ever so much better off, and even the infirm and disabled now had something of a security blanket to wrap round themselves.

Importantly, the mood of the population had changed. The dour acceptance of one's unfortunate fate had gone away. WWI and the Depression left scars and indelible marks, and the mid-1930's were marred by job insecurity and worsening international threat. On top of economic hardship the fear, and then the actuality, of WWII, had haunted the oldies.

But the young men and women who emerged from this war were different. For them, the freedom from the fears of the war, and the restrictions of the war, gave them a realisation that better times were here **now**. **Many of the old taboos were gone forever.**

By the start of 1967, bikini swimsuits were old hat, some people were no longer standing up for the National Anthem in theatres, many women were not wearing stockings and petticoats, people were allowed to gamble in public, hotels were open till late, many sports were played on Sundays and they charged entrance fees, Hire Purchase had removed the tyranny of the banks in lending, and Rock-and-Roll and then the Beatles were disturbing the peace with their performances and riotous audiences.

On a more serious level, **Church attendances were down** and many in the community were feeling emancipated. The fear of God, and the demands of set rituals, were no longer important to them. For them, **God was no longer an angry warder, but had become quite Christian**. Importantly, **blind bigotry**, that had marred the world for centuries, was on the decline. Of course, it still ruined the lives of many, but the thin edge of the wedge was finding cracks.

The white man in Australia was starting to talk about giving the **Aboriginal population** a fair go. **Women** were finding their voices and, as the old model of a man supporting a family of six gave way to everyone for themselves, they were getting closer than before to equal pay for equal work. Importantly, the **contraceptive pill** was now on the scene, and for some women this brought a novel freedom. As I said in my *1965 Conclusion*, "I think women are here to stay."

On the international scene, **China and Vietnam were the nation's biggest worry**. I won't go into detail here because we will hear a lot of these as the year goes on. Suffice to say that our American friends were convinced that the Chinese Reds were intent on winning military victories in all the nations of South East Asia, then Indonesia, Australia, and their ultimate prize, Tasmania. We were one of America's closest allies, and quite prepared to follow her in most matters. So now that the US was seriously putting fighting troops into Vietnam, we too were sending more and more young men to the slaughter in that country. By 1967, our men in the Regular Army and our youths conscripted for National Service were suffering the horrors of war overseas, and increasing numbers were being killed and wounded in **a war that was dividing the nation**. I will not spend time **here** on the passions being raised by **the**

bitter arguments being fought within the nation, but **will come back to them in later pages**.

One overseas factor playing quietly in the background was **the demand in many Third World nations for control over their own destinies**. This was showing up in riots, battles, uprisings, and overthrows of governments, as well as dubious election results. No continent was spared. Again, we will see more evidence of this as we proceed.

The Sunday afternoon barbeque in a million backyards in Australia was not much disturbed by the latter turmoil. We noted it, tut-tutted about it, and chucked another prawn on the barbie. Mostly, we were a long way from all the heat that these events generated, and we would only get involved when they mattered to us. Which, we all hoped, would be never.

When we sum it up, conditions and attitudes were pretty sanguine. Except for the terrible spectre of Vietnam. That might just spoil the barbies. We can only wait and see.

SPECIFIC EVENTS FROM 1966

Early in the year, the nation shrugged its shoulders and said that somehow or other, we had to accept decimal currency. By this time, the arguments in favour of it had passed into history. It might have been that because **the US used dollars and cents, we too should have them**. But against that, the US was stuck with miles and yards. **To be logical, should we stick to them also?** But no, we changed over to decimal there too. In any case, on February 14th, our currency changed, and the distance from Sydney to Newcastle went from 100 miles to 160 kilometers. You might say it was just perception, but I am sure the actual distance increased too.

The Sydney Opera House was in the news all year. The designer Joern Utzon was sacked early in the year and a committee took over to finish off the fine details of design. Could this grand building be truly constructed under a committee? Would it end up looking like the tramsheds it replaced? In any case, how could NSW afford it? Would the nation listen to the Letter-writer from Darwin who asked for a similar building for Darwin? He reckoned that Darwin was a great spot for a concert. Then later in the year, how to finance the cost of the project became an issue. The cost just kept rising and rising. Opera House Lotteries were a bit of a help, but was there any other way? **There was.** More taxes.

Libraries came into the public spotlight. Only a few Councils round the nation had free library services, and then most had only a single outlet for the entire municipality. Most people agreed that free extensive services would be a good thing, but there were the usual concerns about who would pay. If it meant a lift in rates paid to Councils, and it certainly did, was it worth it? In fact the burden of costs fell on owners of properties, because they were the only persons who paid rates. Was this fair to them? All the free-loaders who paid no rates thought the idea of a free library service was a great one. Where could you strike a balance?

When this controversy was dying down, it got fresh legs when the question of who the books should be purchased for was raised. Parents wanted books for their children.

Older women wanted women's books, and older men did not read.

Some people objected that children now had more than enough available to them, and objected to the chocolate finger prints that they left on the *Noddy's*. One woman raised a good point that she had been denied an education in her childhood, and now wanted to catch up. But when she went to a library, all she could get were childrens' books and tear-jerkers. She wanted libraries to first stock all non-fiction books on history and morality, and get the others only when the time was right.

In any case, **free public libraries were a hot issue in 1966.**

Bob Menzies had been Prime Minister for 17 years, and was as comfortable as could be. He controlled the parliamentary votes of his own Liberal Party and also those of Arthur Fadden's Country Party, and he and they had unworried control of the legislation and administration of the nation.

The Opposition was led by Arthur Calwell, who was struggling to gain any sort of traction against the Liberals, and was fighting non-stop to control the factions battling within his own Party. About every second election during Menzies' reign, Labor got reasonably close to gaining power, but had never succeeded since the days of Chifley.

Menzies was a very persuasive and eloquent speaker. **He used his oratory endlessly to berate the Communists.** This well-organised and passionate group of advocates wanted to see a Communist state replace our easy-going democracy, so that it would be **the state** that allocated all resources, owned all property and took all the profits. The profits would then be shared among the workers. In short, they wanted a Communist state, along the lines of Russia or maybe China.

Within the Australian Communist Party, there were two distinct groups. **Firstly**, there were many who wanted to see the transformation to the Red state brought about by violent revolution. That meant the overthrow of the government, **probably the lopping of heads**, and the creation of a bureaucracy that would bring in the ideal state. The key point was that they wanted **a violent revolution** to do this.

Then there was a **second group**, much more moderate, who wanted the changes, but hoped they could make them in **a non-violent manner**. It was alright with them if they could cripple the economy by strikes, if that weakened the government to the point of collapse. That would make possible the creation of a new socialist state.

The two groups came together uneasily into one Party. It never did any good at all in elections in Australia, but by 1966 it had managed to gain control over some of the biggest trade unions. With this control, it sought to undermine the nation's economy by calling strikes.

Thus, the nation was constantly disrupted by strike after strike. Almost always, they were only for a day or two. Occasionally, a major strike might take as much as a month before it broke. It was not so much the duration that troubled the population, it was the number of petty and pointless stoppages across all industries that happened week after week. Once again, I will keep you informed as we go about any major moves in this field, but remember that all citizens were annoyed almost daily by some group of workers who thought that they could create a better world by not working in this one.

OUR AMERICAN ALLIANCE

We in Australia had a choice as to whether we went into the US camp or went with Russia. A few nations, like India, had tried to be neutral and get aid from both sides, but with our heritage and institutions, we went almost thoughtlessly with the US.

Another reason why we had to side with one or the other was that we had such a small population. Clearly, in the belligerent world that had now developed, if we had to defend ourselves, we could not do so with such a small population. So, we had to boost our natural birthrate by taking in lots of migrants.

But that alone would not save us. We needed a big friend, one that carried a big stick. So, we opted for the US. There were quite a few people who said that this was wrong for many reasons. But most people saw it as a realistic defence measure and, perhaps grudgingly, went along with it.

Joining the Alliance, though, had some disadvantages. It meant that we had to stick with American foreign policy, and it is true to say that we did not admire that on all occasions. That meant we had to send our men off to fight and be killed in a few overseas wars, and that we occasionally had to huff and puff against some other nation when the Yanks told us to.

President Johnson had just had a rapid tour Down Under, and that was a good sign that **the Alliance was as steady as a rock**. It was just something that we would have to live with, long term.

MY RULES IN WRITING

Now we are just about ready to go. First, though, I give you a few Rules I follow as I write. They will help you understand where I am coming from.

NOTE. Throughout this book, I rely a lot on reproducing Letters from the newspapers. Whenever I do this, I put the text in a different font, and indent it a little, and make the font somewhat smaller. **I do not edit the text at all**. That is, I do not correct spelling or grammar, and if the text gets at all garbled, I do not correct it. It's just as it was seen in the Papers.

SECOND NOTE. The material for this book, when it comes from newspapers, is reported as it was seen at the time. If the benefit of hindsight over the years changes things, then I **might** record that in my **Comments**. The info reported thus reflects matters **as they were seen in 1967**.

THIRD NOTE. Let me also apologise in advance to anyone I might offend. In a work such as this, it is certain some people will think I got some things wrong. I am sure that I did, but please remember, all of this is **only my opinion**. And really, **my opinion does not matter one little bit in the scheme of things. I hope you will say "silly old bugger", and shrug your shoulders, and read on.**

So now we are ready to plunge into 1967. Let's go, and I trust you will have a pleasant trip.

JANUARY NEWS ITEMS

At Nelson Bay, a coastal town in NSW, two lobster fishermen found that **a pair of swallows had made a nest near their steering wheel**. When the young ones had hatched, the brothers were faced with a dilemma. If they went to sea at the normal crack of dawn, the parent birds would return to the nest with food, and their young ones would not be there....

They decided to **wait two hours each day until the little ones were fed**. They found that their **catches of lobsters were much improved**. It sounds corny, but one of the brothers said "**virtue has its own reward.**"

Our **interstate airlines** were run by just two companies Ansett-ANA and TAA. For example, between Sydney and Melbourne, each flew about six flights a day each way. The trouble was that the two airlines **scheduled departures at the same time**, within 10 minutes of each other. This was to pick up the business peak hours....

This long-standing lack of co-ordination had gone on for a decade. Now, new timetables were issued, **but no changes were made**. The public is just about fed up with this situation, and is talking all the time **about ending this comfortable duopoly**.

Cricket Test Matches were drawing large crowds in Australia. Likewise **in India** where large crowds turned out to see a Test match playing between India and the visiting West Indies. Some of them jumped the fence, to sit on the fringes of the field. Police moved them back...

But tempers were raised, missiles were thrown, police were punched, the players left the field, chairs and fencing were brought onto the pitch and burned, and bamboo stakes were driven into the pitch. Police were driven from the ground, and **after that** a full scale riot ensued. Play was officially cancelled for the day....

Not exactly the quiet day that Members could expect at grounds round Australia.

Donald Campbell, holder of various land and water speed records, **was killed in another attempt to set a water speed record in England**. His *Bluebird* vessel left the water and crashed at a speed of 310 miles per hour, and sank with him strapped into his seat....

Campbell was well known in Australia for his number of attempts to break the land speed record a few years earlier. It seemed he was always close to the record, but was **frustrated by unlikely rains, and the flooding of Lake Eyre on a few occasions**. He epitomised **the daredevil gentleman**, charming and handsome and patriotic, rich and idle, **who nevertheless achieved remarkable feats**.

If you are a bit worried about a nice day at the cricket, **why not try Sydney's beaches?** The sand blowing in your face, the water icy cold, the young men posturing in front of sun-burned bikini-clad nubiles. Sounds great? But for one trouble. **The beaches are being invaded by blue-bottles.** Last Sunday, 3,000 people **reported** being stung, sometimes with cramps and vomiting. **Not so great!**

BACKGROUND TO VIETNAM

The fighting in Vietnam was an ideological battle between Capitalism and Communism. The Capitalists were mainly America and its allies such as Australia, backed up by the people of South Vietnam. The Communists were an undisclosed mixture of Reds, some of them Chinese, backed up by the people and government of North Vietnam. **Both sides** to the war said that they had the best system of everything, that they could run the world better than the other side, and that they could win more wars.

Of course, it was all mixed up with **lots and lots of propaganda**. In Australia, we were told that the Reds wanted to capture all the dominoes from Vietnam right down to Tasmania. We were told that they were inhuman monsters, that they would stop at nothing, that danger to us was always pressing, and that the might of the full Chinese Army was poised ready to enter the fray if we didn't manage to scare them off. The Reds were told similar things about the US and its allies, and were just as convinced as we were that **they** were the goodies.

The battle between the two sides was waging backward and forward. The military forces of North Vietnam were partly government sponsored, and partly by **a Communist group, called the Viet Cong**. It is this latter group that was at the forefront of the attacks on the South.

The war had been getting more and more serious for over a year. Australia had been sending troops and advisers for most of the time, and many of these were young babies, conscripted at the age of 20 years, who mostly had no idea of where Vietnam was before they were drafted.

Public opinion at the moment was polarised into **two groups**. **The first**, following the American and Bob Menzies' line, thought that the Reds worldwide were a menace that would threaten everything that the Western democracies stood for. It was their argument that, unless the Reds were now stopped in Vietnam, they would continue on and take over nation after nation, and establish world domination along Communist lines.

The second group did not believe any of this. They thought that the battle in Vietnam was originally part of a world-wide movement to **get rid of oppressive foreign colonial powers**, and that the wily Reds had harnessed these nationalist forces into military groups intent on removing the foreigners. This group argued that once the locals got their independence, they would chuck out the Communists as well, and not be at all concerned with the world around them.

In the background, however, were capitalist America and the Chinese Reds who were driven by ideological motives. Each wanted to prove how good their political system was, and how utterly bad was the other political system.

So, it was a mixed bag of combatants. Early in 1967, there was something of a military stalemate, and it would be silly to give you any more details because it would all change

Let me just say that our Australian lads, and also the Regular Army troops, were being killed at about a dozen or more a week, and millions of Australians were convinced that this was an absolutely wrong cause to be fighting for. Part of society here was bitterly opposing every move to continue, or even escalate, the war, and were holding demonstrations and marches day after day. But they were being **met by equal numbers of those who thought winning the war was our only and last hope**, and who were prepared to take to the streets in demonstrations to espouse that cause.

So we start 1967 with a nation that was bitterly and actively divided. **Everything else was pretty good.** The Baby Boom has just finished, and the tots were growing up to be little nuisances filled with their own self-importance. Their slowly aging parents, moaning a lot about the demise of the good old days, nevertheless knew full well that they were on a better wicket that any generation of Australians before had ever been.

So the only ointment fly of any size was the Vietnam war. As we proceed, I will obviously talk more about this, though at this stage I expect to stay away from the military side of it, and talk mainly about its social impact. Let's see how well I can stick to that, given that the news services are full of it day and night.

But just before **I move on to current news events and opinions,** I will give you a longish Letter that delves into the reasons that many Americans (and some Australians) had for supporting the Vietnam war. It was from a Lecturer at Brisbane University.

Letters, Edmond Earl. There are many reasons given for US involvement in Vietnam. All of these give a single simple reason, whereas the true reason is complex and ever-changing. Let me explain.

Some people would support the American action there because they believe that the Reds are a threat to South East Asia, and the Pacific. They remember Hitler, and think that if he had been stopped early,

then there would have been no WWII. Others think
that the only way to defeat Communism world-wide is
to beat it militarily. This is an ideological perspective,
deep-seated in a long-term hatred of the threat of
Communism to the perfection of Capitalism.

Others see it as an opportunity to spread Christianity.
Another powerful group wants to sell massive quantities
of arms and munitions. Many in the armed forces hope
to get rapid promotion in wartime. Some few resent **all**
Asian influence in the USA and the world.

Manufacturers of **all** goods see marketing opportunities
if Asia is Americanised. Politicians, wrapping themselves
in the flag, are counting the votes that will come with
every bit of good news.

In fact, I could go on and on. So for people to say that
there is **a single reason** for involvement is very **naïve
and dangerously deceptive**.

I add that all of this will change with time. At the moment,
the war is getting support (far from unanimous, though)
from most Americans. This will change with time.
As more Americans are killed, when the propaganda
machine has to tell of mounting American losses,
and as the scale of the bombings of Vietnam citizens
become known, some of these groups above will drift to
opposing the war.

Anyway, beware of those who say the Yanks are in for
just one single reason. **Your speaker** may have just
one reason, but the **nation** has many reasons.

DO WE LIKE ASIANS?

Of course, 22 years after the war ended, we certainly do
not like the Japanese. So we should keep them out of this
discussion. But what about those Asians nations that gave
us invaluable support during the war? And what about
those that are members of the British Empire? Surely there

is no reason not to like them. Some people were suggesting that they **now** should be allowed to migrate to this wide white land. That is not the question I am asking here. My question is, whether we should like them **in any way?**

One Letter-writer did not mince his words. He was incensed by an Editorial in the *SMH* that said that we should now adopt a policy of mateship with Asia and be happy to offer any assistance consistent with that mateship. He gave the *SMH* a full blast.

Letters, F Charlton. As for your statement that the real challenge to "mateship" now lies in Asia, I beg to differ most vehemently. If anybody in this country nourishes the mistaken idea that there will ever be any "mateship" between Australians (or any white race) and Asiatics, however close the geographical position, he can take it from me, and thousands of others who have had contact with them, that no truer phrase was ever written than "...never the twain shall meet."

Despite the pleas by newspapers and the politicians and petty sentimentalists, there is never a single thought expressed about the true position regarding the starvation and poverty in India and part of Asia.

Therefore I wish to bring to the minds of thinking Australians a thought which never should be forgotten: I refer to the great and indisputable fact that the poverty-stricken peoples of Asia today have been on this earth just as long as the prosperous whites - longer, if you can believe some of their claims to "ancient civilisation" - but most of them still haven't brains enough to produce enough food to keep themselves alive, to produce machinery to cultivate the earth, in fact insufficient grey matter to produce anything of a worthwhile nature in this modern world.

The only thing they produce, ever, is unwanted offspring at the rate of so many per second and, with nothing to feed them on, they cry out to the whites for succour in the form of powdered milk, flour, wheat, rice.

What we should send them is a book of recipes on how to make billions of anti-birth pills and then, when they get their birthrate down below manageable level, we could send them some blueprints on how to manufacture modern food-producing machinery. If they fail, then, to lift themselves up from the status of common beggars, let them starve and we'll all be better off because the wealth we now pour down the drains in Asia could be distributed among our own needy people, and, believe me, there are thousands of them.

Never will I donate one cent towards improving conditions in the vast Asian slum you refer to - and I implore all Australians to adopt this attitude, this same policy, while ever there is one needy Australian man, woman or child in our country.

As you might expect, there were more than a few responses.

Letters, Barbara Coleman, James Masselos, Sydney University. The chauvinistic fear of Asian hordes is one that has dogged Australia's history, while the strangeness of Asian cultures has been a constant preoccupation of Western man since he came into contact with the East.

Charlton's hypothetical "thousands" notwithstanding, "mateship" between Asians and Australians is not only possible but does exist. At the personal level, from our own experience in one case as a social worker, and in the other as a research student in one Asian country, India, we can affirm that "mateship" between Australians and Asiatics is a reality, a reality which was as true for ourselves as for our other Western friends in similar situations. The basis of such relationships is a willingness to "give and take" and to respect attitudes different from one's own.

Mr Charlton would have us believe that the "whites", through the working of some form of providence, are inherently superior, that they are totally free from corruption and have always, and invariably, been prosperous. The idea of racial superiority is one that should have disappeared with Nazi Germany, while the presence of black markets in the West is of too recent a memory to provide a sound argument. Regarding prosperity, let us remember that until the nineteenth century it was Asia that was wealthy and the leader in manufactures, that until World War II a country like India was a surplus food exporter, and that she, with other nations, fed Britain.

Mr Charlton is correct when he maintains that population control is one of the urgent necessities in the Asian situation. This is a fact of which most Asian Governments are aware. But birth-control programs are by their very nature long-term remedies.

However, the current situation in Asia also requires immediate short-term remedies. In a country such as India, where drought and famine have struck two years in succession, the need is even more desperate. India at the moment urgently requires large quantities of aid, both food and machinery, to prevent mass starvation in Bihar and Uttar Pradesh. In such circumstances any kind of aid, large and small, is of vital importance. It is not enough to rationalise and maintain that aid should not be given because of the possible existence of corruption or inefficiency of distribution.

Ways and means do exist to channel aid to the worst-affected areas and to ensure its proper utilisation. One such avenue is the Aid to India campaign, which to date has sent 670 tons of processed milk to India. The chairman has authorised us to appeal, on behalf of Aid to India, for financial donations with which to purchase bulk packed powdered milk. Such powdered milk will be offered to the Government of India for immediate distribution to the near-starving people of Bihar and Uttar Pradesh.

There were quite a few Letters that supported this Christian approach, but not everyone went so quietly.

Letters, John McDonald. I could not agree more with the uncharitable expressions of F Charlton concerning the need for Indians to operate on a self-help basis instead of whining for succour from the rest of the world. Whatever may be said about Communist China, one does not hear that sort of thing from them. When they want wheat, they buy it in hard cash, and a lot of Australian farmers would be out of business if they did not adopt this policy.

WELL, *MATE*, WHAT ABOUT FILIPINOS?

Suppose we did open our hearts to Asians and send them aid, should we open our borders too. It might have benefits for all concerned, said this writer.

Letters, W Cammack, MB, BS. The Australian Dental Association has referred to the admission of Filipino dentists as a solution to the shortage of dentists here.

As an observer-delegate to the recent World Medical Association Congress in Manila, I was asked on a number of occasions by Filipino doctors, and by an architect, why Australia will not permit them to migrate and practise here. Many of them, as well as other Asians, go to America, some to specialise after higher qualifications and later return to their own country, and some to practise there.

While this is something of a loss to the Philippines (and that country needs doctors for the outback, too), I feel we could relax our immigration laws and arrange registration for those suitable professionals who wish to migrate. Dr George Swinbourne, an Australian Medical Association delegate and Federal Councillor, has undertaken, in a private capacity, to raise the matter in official circles.

Filipino doctors (and all I met were most delightful people) could well help to solve our own shortage problem. And what is more, they all speak English.

Comment. At the moment, there were hundreds of doctors and dentists who had migrated to Australia from England and Europe and were in various stages of applying for citizenship. But most of these, despite excellent credentials from overseas, could not get accreditation to practise in Australia. Our professions were, not unreasonably, intent on keeping a lid on the number of practitioners, and had set rules and regulations so as to limit any influx from overseas.

The idea that we give entry to numbers of qualified Asians, even with good qualifications, was asking too much.

WHAT DO WE THINK OF AFRICAN BLACKS?

Continuing with the theme of our relationships with overseas coloured races, the Letter below presents a perspective that contradicts many of our long-held images.

Letters, D Baillie. As a Rhodesian of mature age and travelling around your beautiful country, I have been hurt many times by the harsh terms in which many Australians describe my country. I would like to point out a few of the facts to them.

First, we have 15 black members of Parliament, who have the same privileges as the whites. All bus drivers and postmen are blacks - taxidrivers, too. No white is allowed to run a taxi, although representation has been made to our Government to allow this. There are bank clerks and post-office clerks who are black and many hundreds of small shops throughout the country are owned by our black brothers. We even have one millionaire among them who owns shops and a string of buses.

The old fable of the black being made to walk in the gutter is about as true as the one that all Australians are descended from convicts. I might add that there are hundreds of schools throughout Rhodesia, either Government or missionary-run, for the black African and that two-thirds of the students at Salisbury University are coloured people. Those trouble-makers who riot and throw petrol bombs into cafes, those who murder innocent farmers and their wives are Communist-trained, as is evident by the capture by our troops of Chinese and Russian-made machine-guns and hand-grenades.

This has been confirmed by my own son now in the armed forces. We do not seek financial aid from Britain, but many British and American firms have invested in Rhodesia and more are building factories there at this present time.

I hope these few facts may cast a little light on conditions in my small country.

Comment. This Letter applies to Rhodesia only, I assume. But the woman writer has described the impression that Australians currently had about blacks in **all** Africa. If the writer was to be successful in changing **this**, she would have a long hard road ahead of her.

FEBRUARY NEWS ITEMS

Ronald Ryan was hanged in Melbourne. He had been **convicted of murder** after he escaped from prison and killed a warder in doing so. That was in 1965, and since then "Victoria has been in a turmoil of protest, marches, violence, accusations, Court appeals, and thundering newspaper editorials, **splitting the community into bitterly divided groups**"....

Despite that, there were **only 1,000 protestors** outside the prison when the execution took place. The *SMH* said that while the majority of the population were against capital punishment, there was still a vocal minority that supported it....

It expected the matter to lie dormant in Victoria for a few months when three men and a woman are also sentenced to death. **Will the fact that a woman is involved make a difference?**....

In fact, **their sentences were commuted** and the matter was laid to rest. **Ronald Ryan was the last person to be executed in Australia.**

President Ky, of South Vietnam, has returned home after being in Australia for much of January. Everywhere he went there were **demos against him**, and near-riots in some places. Despite being the leader of a friendly power, and being feted by the Government, there was no sign of **the ordinary citizen** here **extending him the courtesies** normally given to Heads of State.

Tasmania was **the latest State to suffer from bushfires**. Probably 50 people are dead, "we haven't had time to count the corpses", said a constable. 450 houses were completely destroyed near Hobart. It happens every year in some part of Australia. **Comment.** We need to do more than cleaning out our gutters.

Russian Chess Master, Yuri Averbakh, squared off against **43 top-rated chess enthusiasts at the same time** in Canberra yesterday. In **a six hour session**, he defeated 36, drew with six, and lost to one. **He walked two and a half miles in doing this.** He spent an average of 10 minutes with each player....

He has played about **500 exhibition games** since he came to Australia three weeks ago.

Professional tennis has arrived in Australia. Jack Kramer's "travelling circus" played matches in Sydney before moderate crowds. **This new form of competition it still on the nose with the amateurs**, where the lily-whites are refusing any contact with the pros....

Kramer's band of about eight players is travelling the world and rewarding each player with cash if he wins a match against another band-member. The *SMH* said **that the clash between the amateurs and the pros must come to a head soon.**

Comment. When it did, slowly over years, pure amateur tennis disappeared, so now **all good performers play for money.** Over the same time, **Kramer's troupe lost its appeal** and is now very minor in the scheme of things.

Jack Ruby, the man who apparently **shot US President Kennedy, died of cancer.** He had been in prison, awaiting a new trail for the murder.

KIDS EVERYWHERE

It is now 22 years since the end of WWII, and the chickens bred then are coming home to roost. More accurately, the first lot of Baby Boomers are aged about 20, and there are teenagers seemingly all over the place.

All of these were pumped full of nonsense from the media and advertisers saying that they were the greatest generation ever. And maybe they were at that, but in any case, they were a vast swarm of little blighters given more freedom than any generation before them had ever had, and with enough money and hot-rods to indulge in behaviours that free young spirits can devise.

Most of these were harmless. But not all. So that there was a growth in anti-social behaviour, often in gangs, like crime and bashings. Taxi drivers were favoured targets, while drunks in parks were also popular. Poofters were sought out and encouraged to go straight, while fights between football gangs were very common.

In fact, there were no knives or guns most of the time, and apart from the above obvious targets, their behaviour was more frightening than real.

Still, the Papers were full of reports of bad behaviour and of course, lots of Letters. For example, every State had much public discussion about the roles that police should adopt, and the causes of the malaise and the remedies. And, of course, how the miscreants should be punished.

A typical Letter below talks about **only one side of the problem**. That was the perceived need to remove protections on **the naming of juveniles in Court reports**.

Letters, Marien Dreyer. For some years past I was a solitary voice predicting violence in the streets unless more police were used in Sydney. I was - because of this - publicly spat at in the street, suffered (and still suffer) obscene telephone calls and was once told, "Watch out you don't get a knife in your ribs." These events did not silence me - but the apathy of the Police Commissioner and State Government make me feel it was wasted time.

Any observant person could see what was developing with the illiterate, mentally and spiritually bankrupt children of this era. I say "illiterate" because many of them **are** - as any employment officer of any firm will know.

As it seems that the Police Commissioner can only wring his hands in dismay and do nothing, and the State Government is even less able to control the situation, may I suggest that the laws relating to the Children's Court be amended to **allow the publication of names of offenders**?

The present situation is that minors shelter behind a closed court. Publish the names of the offenders and their parents suffer neighbourhood criticism and ostracism. Add an additional clause that parents of minors convicted of vandalism and assault must pay damages for the errors of the children, and I think the results would justify the amendments. Few things have a more salutary effect than the acid comments of neighbours and relations, and what they don't achieve, making the parents pay would.

Any minor who is allowed to run wild is old enough to face the consequences, and parents who don't care what their children do should be made to pay for their sins of omission and know what people think of them. Even if it means that, at long last, parents decide to use

applied child psychology - preferably with a razor-strop to the seat of the tight, blue jeans.

Letters, M Dwyer. At the moment, I believe, minors aged under 18 have closed-court protection. **The age limit should be reduced to 16**, so that boys and girls who act like delinquent adults, and worse, should suffer justice in its full maturity.

Like Marien Dreyer, I think the glare of publicity would do a lot towards curbing this State's crop of louts and hooligans.

There were, as usual, other sides to the story.

Letters, L Wilkins. One section of the Sydney Press is busily criticising the Police Force for what it describes as "kid glove" treatment of hooligans and louts.

But the same section is always to the forefront in demands for Royal Commissions or "independent" inquiries whenever there is the slightest suggestion that police officers meted out anything other than "kid glove" treatment to young offenders.

No wonder members of the Police Force declare openly that they are "browned off" because of continued unfair and uninformed criticism. Anti-police campaigns of this unreasonable nature neither help the public nor the morale of the police.

They are certainly harmful to the current police recruiting drive.

Letters, Margaret Forrest. Most thinking people will agree with Marien Dreyer in her contention that some kind of new approach is needed to the problem of hoodlum attacks on helpless people in particular and the official attitude to youthful delinquency in general. I share her concern but do not agree in full with her solutions.

I could not agree more with her criticism of a Police Commissioner who, living in an ivory tower, is quite aloof from the problems faced by both citizens and the unfortunate rank and file in the Police Force.

I do not share in her feeling that blame should be pinpointed on parents, because parents have been so completely confused by **the muddled attitude of much-publicised psychiatrists** whose constant theme is that "**there are no delinquent children, only delinquent parents**."

The truth is that there is both good and bad in people of all ages and to focus all blame on parents does more harm than good. Certain shrewd young people learn that they will always get a good official hearing just so long as they keep blaming mum and dad for everything. Bewildered parents with difficult children find that, no matter what they do, they are wrong. If they are lenient and loving, as told to be, and a child goes astray, then they spoilt the child and were not firm enough. If they dare to try severer methods and the child still goes astray then it is because he was beaten.

I believe it would be a good thing if the closed court for juveniles were flung wide open and for more reasons than mentioned by Marien Dreyer. At least an open court securely establishes the identities of the true offenders and there is no possibility of inaccurate rumours, which involve innocent juveniles, gaining credence. At present no one knows from all the numerous noisy and vociferous young people around just who are the villains and who are the completely harmless exhibitionists just passing through a noisy stage. Gossip and rumour tend always to brand the innocent.

Many parents with somewhat exhibitionist but basically sound children have had experiences that could not have arisen but for a closed court system.

At least open courts would provide the public with the truth both as to the extent of juvenile thuggery and so on, and also as to the exact identity of those engaging in it.

Comment. There were of course, different views of the problem. As we saw, one theme that always comes out in such discussions is that it is not the offenders who are at fault, but rather their parents. And another popular theme is that the indirect cause is that youth is subjected to pornographic literature, to obscene movies, and even girlie photos in newspapers. Then again psychologists will talk about sex offenders in particular, and then come up with a mixed bag of causes and remedies.

My point here is that while teenage deviance is not new, **the scale** of it now was completely new. And so too was **the acceptance of it by much of the juvenile population.** Previous generations had been shamed by anti-social conduct. But the current mobs of teenagers saw some **form of rebellion** as the only way to go. Fortunately, as I mentioned earlier, their activities were in fact not so bad. But the spectre of them **frightened** many parents and teachers and schools **that had memories of regimented teenage years, and feared that society would collapse in the face of the exercise of excess freedoms.**

THE HANGING OF RONALD RYAN

Ronald Ryan's death was deplored by the *SMH*.

Editorial. One may concede that there is still a substantial minority which sincerely believes, in the face of all the evidence to the contrary, in the value of the death penalty as a deterrent to murder. There are others who would at least retain it for those cases, like this one, where a policeman or a warder has been killed in the course of his duty, though - and this must be emphasised - no such distinction is made in the law as it now stands in Victoria. But even Sir Henry Bolte will surely admit that when the community is so deeply divided on this issue, when the prospect of a hanging arouses such deep and violent opposition, to retain the death penalty does far more harm to the idea of justice than any possible advantage it may have as a deterrent.

Debates about capital punishment were not new. Over the first 67 years of the Century, the number of persons hanged had dropped, until now only a few were actually executed. So these flare-up debates had decreased in number.

But when they caught the public attention, they were fierce and bitter. Arguments abounded. For example, Christian morality said that **human life was sacrosanct**, yet the Bible talked about an eye for an eye. **The cost of keeping a prisoner for life** in gaol was weighed against the prospect of a wrongful decision. The **likelihood of reform**, the death penalty for **just one moment of violence**, the question of **sanity**, the **effect on family**, all were argued back and forth with no one ever changing their opinion.

So, the Editorial from the *SMH* unearthed dozens of responses that showed once again that society had not changed all that much from earlier years.

Letters, M Zell. In considering the merits and demerits of capital punishment, as put forward by your correspondents, it is irritating to come across that stupid but often repeated phrase, "it has not been proved that capital punishment has acted as a deterrent to murder."

Of course it hasn't been proved! The only proof which would satisfy the makers of such statements would be to produce some person, or persons, who were willing to admit that they had contemplated murder, but had been deterred from so doing by fear of the death penalty. **Is it likely that such a person would come forward?** I am prepared to admit that there are some people whom nothing would deter - flogging, death penalty or anything else - but he would be very naive indeed - and singularly lacking in knowledge of human nature - who would seriously maintain that no one had been deterred from committing murder.

However, it is certain that **capital punishment does prevent the murderer from again killing anyone else**, for it is reasonable to assume that having once killed he would again do so in the same circumstances.

Letters, E Bartlett. Even so, it is safe to say that it will be a long time before the death penalty is legislated out of the laws of every British community. The mystery is that any Christian country should have tolerated this penalty so long - or at any rate should have retained the grim words which it is the duty of every Judge in British courts to recite whenever the death sentence is passed.

These words are unnecessarily barbaric in the passing of a sentence which, in these enlightened times, is barbaric in itself.

Letters, John Lanser. The *SMH* editorial contention that only a "substantial minority" still believes in the death penalty is, I suggest, wishful thinking. Polls on the question are, regrettably, only taken at times when an execution is imminent, and the outcome usually depends upon the nature of the condemned criminal and his crime.

Monsters like John Christie (and, more recently, the moors murderers) evoke an upsurge of "ayes" for the death penalty, whereas pathetic figures like Derek Bentley (a mental defective executed in Britain in 1953 for complicity in the murder of a policeman) augment the "nays."

All this proves that the public's attitude to capital punishment is largely based on emotion, so it is surely the duty of the Press to exert a countervailing intellectual influence. Yet the current sickening hysteria has contributed most to making the Ryan case, as your editorial has it, "downright farcical." Headlines have made the hero Ryan himself.

This sort of propaganda generates more heat than light, and the cause of justice and reason will best be served by saying first to those responsible, "Enough."

Letters, Harold Brown. The "Herald's" editorial on the decision to hang Ryan was interesting, but did not help to face the fact that a jury found him guilty of killing the warder. In my opinion, he did it to obtain his freedom and would go to any length to gain that end. He had a criminal record and has been a burden on the public for a long time and does not deserve any sympathy.

Has the public who opposed the hanging any thought or sympathy for the warder and his family?

Comment. I wonder, if the matter was put in 2020 to a referendum, how the Australian public would vote. Would they adopt the civilised approach and vote against it? Or would they say that in some cases the "bastard deserves everything he gets"?

Or would the result depend on the timing? What if it were put **just after** some horrific crime involving children had shocked the nation?

Second Comment. I leave it to you to decide. For myself, I expect the nation would vote soberly against the death penalty, but not by a big majority.

A MAN IN CLERGY'S CLOTHING

In this emancipated world of 1967, it seemed that everyone was demanding that they be relieved of some restrictions that had been imposed on them previously. Even our mild-mannered clergy were sometimes getting into this modern-day thinking, and a few were being quite daring in their own way.

They were saying that they wanted to be relieved of wearing their dog-collar. There was little suggestion that they wanted to be relieved of it **all** the time, but when the occasion was appropriate, why not, they argued, take off their collars and run free as the wind? Or something like that.

At the moment, in conservative parishes, the Bishop or local Church authority forbade it. In other, more permissive regions, the idea was catching on, and getting support from some of the flock. But there were reservations.

Letters, (Mrs) Mildred Staker. One can understand the attitude that "A priest should appear to be what he is" school of thought, but there are many cases when a priest, dressed as an ordinary citizen, can further the causes of Christianity in the outside world and help people more easily than if he was dressed as a priest.

The very people who need the help of a man of the Church often give him a wide berth because of his clerical garb. The elevation and dignity of his office and, as they think, isolation from everyday living seem emphasised by the uniform of his calling.

Surely those who like to see their holy men suitably labelled and packaged could settle for him appearing so in church and **leave it to his own discretion** as to whether he wears the garb in the outside world. Dignitaries of other callings do not have to wear their official robes outside of the place of their taking up their status position. One such dignitary is the Judge. Another the lawyer or barrister.

Just imagine if everyone demanded they parade the streets appearing to be what they are. Then we would have professors walking about in their robes, nurses likewise, etc., etc. A man is no less a professor, Judge or whatever you like to name, without his robes. In fact as regards the clergy he can probably follow his most important role - that of helping human beings who need help - when he is dressed as an ordinary man. His robes are merely robes of office.

Letters, Sheila Whiteway. I have read with interest comments for and against the wearing of clerical garb when priests are not officiating in church.

First, in my own experience as an Anglo-Catholic, there is nothing more annoying than to answer the front door to be greeted by a person who is obviously posing as someone else. It does seem that many clerical gentlemen in this diocese seem to be ashamed of their vocation in the heritage of the Church of England.

If a priest is doing his job properly, he will be accepted anywhere in his "dog collar," whether it be in a home, at the races or at the local hotel, and there is no doubt that people do feel deceived when they realise that they have been talking to a priest in disguise. The wearing of official robes by Judges, lawyers, etc, is quite irrelevant, as they are not likely to be calling at the front door to inquire if one has made a will, or what have you.

Secondly, it is a fallacy to say that it is too hot in this climate to wear clerical clothing. Many priests have told me that a cassock and collar is much cooler to wear than a suit, collar and tie.

Surely it is only the rigid evangelical outlook in this diocese that is urging these changes, as nobody seems to be debating the issue in any other diocese or in other parts of the Anglican Communion, where not only do priests wear clerical garb, but also wear vestments when celebrating Communion.

This may seem a very trite argument, but I think that it is time that many Anglicans were made to feel proud of their apostolic heritage instead of trying to hide it, and this will not be achieved by wearing a collar and tie and by "hell fire" preaching!

Comment. The habit of not having a habit has grown. The most obvious place to see this is in the garb of nuns who quite often appear in public, in incredibly dowdy clothes, nevertheless in civvies rather than habits. They usually sport a very big Crucifix that leaves no doubt as to their vocation but, to my mind, makes them more approachable and credible as citizens of the same world that most of us live in.

NEWS AND VIEWS

Letters, John Dooley. Tourists to New Zealand should be aware that through that Government's carelessness they could lose money on return to Australia. More than 200 tourists during January returned to Australia with NZ currency in handbags and pockets only to discover that no bank or NZ agency could exchange the NZ currency for Australian currency.

Had the NZ Government advised them by a printed note or other positive means, these tourists could have arranged the exchange before departure from NZ. I received no such warning and apparently neither did the 200 others caught during January. (This number was estimated by the bank officer at Kingsford Smith Airport currency exchange office). There was no warning given over the Wellington Airport public address system, nor was mention made by any Customs officer which, I have since been informed, should be done.

Tourists innocently possessing NZ currency need to hawk it around among departing tourists to NZ, or maybe exchange it at low rate with profiteering shopkeepers. The NZ Government Tourist Department should realise that this final sour taste must detract in many cases from an otherwise beautiful tour, and should therefore ensure in future that every tourist is positively informed in regard to NZ currency in Australia.

CHANGES AT THE TOP

The leadership of the Labor Party has changed. Arthur Calwell has gone, and **Gough Whitlam has succeeded**. At long last, **the Labor Party will have a chance of winning back the support of its old stalwarts** who had been shaking their heads at Calwell's espousal of lost causes.

MARCH NEWS ITEMS

Prince Phillip, the Duke of Edinburgh, is in Australia and hob-nobbing with our leading politicians. After a televised Press Conference in Canberra, a reporter commented that **Phillip was a "bloody bore".** This was picked up by a microphone, and **broadcast to the general public. Swearing on the** *ABC*? **God forbid....**

Switchboards on ABC stations were jammed by people complaining, The *ABC* issued directives to other Channels to delete the phrase, and cut it from all re-broadcasts. The *SMH* said that thankfully the Duke did not hear the "swear word." **Phew, that would have been terrible.**

A new dispute was in its infancy. Would butter be replaced by margarine? A visiting US Professor said that while he agreed that eating quantities of butter would cause heart attacks, a 50-50 mixture of butter and margarine would be safe....

This was a compromise position (that pleased no one) in the looming battle over the future of butter. The likelihood of **heart attacks** was the prevailing argument from one side, and the counter claim talked about concepts such as **nature's goodness in butter**. This was a battle where, over 50 years, the arguments from both sides got more scientific or more persuasive, but **has never been settled. Our dairy industry at the time was intensely interested.**

The Seamens' Union made itself unpopular with the Government and the people of Australia. No one takes any notice of their constant strikes most of the time, but **they have just refused to man the cargo ships** *Boonaroo* **and** *Jeparit*. Both of these were due to **sail to Vietnam carrying supplies, guns, and ammunition for our armed forces there....**

It is one thing to go on strike but another to **leave our fighting forces without the materials for survival.** Our navy was ordered **to step in** and take any action necessary, but **the ordinary citizen was appalled....**

Even people who do not want the war to continue do not want to see our men at risk in this way. So **the Union is in the spotlight. How will it react?**

The US Air Force reported a small jungle village in Vietnam had **accidentally** been bombed and that **105 people had been killed.** The two fighter planes involved **straffed the village for 25 minutes,** and dropped the "effective" cluster-bombs, and **the increasingly popular napalm....**

It added that the 2,000 tribesmen and their families were **still huddled in their bunkers, frightened to come out.**

Sorting machines have been **successfully introduced** into our postal system. The trial location at Sydney's Redfern has passed performance tests, and apart from some early hiccups, is working well. **It is not "tearing letters to confetti" as some opponents claim....**

Many of the Unions have opposed its introduction, knowing full well that **job losses would follow.** This is another example of the dreaded **"automation" that was threatening all jobs.**

NO GAOL FOR SUICIDE

The Victorian Government has removed penalties for persons attempting to commit suicide. Let me state the obvious that any one who is successful will not be penalised. But the new rule is that someone who is not successful will no longer be penalised for attempting it.

In fact, **rarely** in any State has that charge actually been laid recently. But the *SMH* says that the legislation is welcome because it brings the law itself into line with actual practice. It urges NSW to do the same.

Note though that some life insurance policies still contain clauses that say that **the policy lapses if the holder commits suicide**. Such provisions still impose a penalty on the successful completion of the act.

SCOUTS AND GUIDES

Many readers of the book will have been a boy scout or girl guide. At the moment, they were thriving. One reason for this was that parents could see that their activities provided an alternative to the destructive pursuits of the bands of hooligans that were so common.

Somewhere in my own memory I can remember being woken by a regular radio 6am message that sang:

Be a good scout, be loyal clean and brave,
Never say die, just chase your blues away,
You must always do your best
When they put you to the test,
So always be a good scout.

It is hard to imagine that any organisation with such a wholesome approach to life could stir up any opposition. But opposition there was.

The cause of this was growing resentment against local Councils giving away control of their land to various groups that wanted to use them for their own selfish purposes. For example, week after week, some protest group wrote to the Press complaining that a new bowling club had been granted Council land, under a 99-year lease. Or a cricket or football club. Or a kindergarten.

It was of course nice for the Councils to have these clubs provide them with revenue. But the alienation of public lands for private purposes was meeting with opposition. .Thus **the scouts were under attack** as they too were given permission to build club houses.

The following Letters were typical

Letters, Eleanor Johnson. Mosman Council, after many years, has at last made some progress towards replacing the eyesore of the boats at Pearl Bay with an attractive park by reclaiming the foreshores. Now we find this new parkland, created at great expense to ratepayers, is not to be left for their use. Large sections of it have already been apportioned to Mosman Rowing Club and a Sea Scouts group.

Both these organisations are comfortably housed elsewhere in the municipality, but this free gift of choice real estate to the Sea Scouts is a most glaring example of official generosity gone wild. There were nine Scout groups in Mosman until one closed recently from lack of members. The Sea Scout group now claiming an exclusive piece of public land at Pearl Bay has, in fact, moved into the Balmoral premises of the closed group, where it could well remain, as part of the building is already used by a sailing club. Just why Mosman municipality must support eight separate Scout groups, when advertisements in the local paper show all eight are half-empty, we are not told.

Does a local council have the authority Mosman Council has assumed, to alienate the use of this public land which the ratepayers' funds are creating? Does the Minister for Lands have any say, since the reclaimed area will apparently become part of an already proclaimed reserve?

Letters, Monty Smith, Bruce Sinclair, Scoutmasters. We wish to reply to Eleanor Johnson's letter regarding the proposed use by the 1st Beauty Point Sea Scouts of a site in Pearl Bay.

(1) This Scout group, and all others, are public bodies. We accept and train for citizenship all boys who desire to join. As such, we are a direct amenity to the ratepayers and to the public, and are in no way a sectional or exclusive group.

(2) This group, and other groups in Mosman, are vigorously working to avoid the development of a hoodlum element and to train boys with higher ideals. It is as much due to the existence of eight Scout groups in Mosman as to any other cause that this suburb has not become an "asphalt jungle" and that our residents can still walk the streets of their suburb in safety and enjoyment. The presence of an active Scout group in Pearl Bay will have a direct and specific effect in making this area less attractive to undesirable elements which the new park is likely to attract from other areas.

(3) Neither the Mosman Rowing Club nor the 1st Beauty Point Sea Scouts have ever been "comfortably housed" as Mrs Johnson suggests. In fact, we have operated as a Scout group for 12 years without premises at all, and

present housing is quite temporary and unsatisfactorily located for the boys it serves.

(4) Far from "giving away" property, Mosman Council has consistently put ratepayers' interests well ahead of those of our group. The council is obliging us to provide standards of building considerably higher than is necessary for our own Scouting purposes in order to meet the aesthetic requirements of the area. We accept and support the Council's desires in this matter.

Letters, V Fairfax, Chief Commissioner, Aust. Boy Scouts' Assn. I believe municipal councils consider Scouting and Guiding as specially essential elements in our social structure and in the same light as other organisations concerned with religion, education and moral upbringing. Aldermen are generally better attuned to the needs of the local communities than most of us. They join you in applauding and respecting the Boy Scout Movement, but they go further and give us much practical help and understanding and encouragement.

I would suggest that by providing unobtrusive and controlled facilities for Scouts they are accurately interpreting the wishes of the majority of their ratepayers and the needs of the community.

In doing this they may run foul of those who are entitled to press with single-minded determination the general cause of conservation of parklands - a cause which I am confident the Boy Scouts will sensibly support now and also when they become responsible adult citizens.

Letters, Caroline Simpson. The number of applicants squabbling for building sites on Crown or council-owned playing field and park land is staggering and must be trying for councillors to decide which group is the most deserving.

I can visualise a park in 50 years' time with an Anglican Scout building up one end and another denominational group of Scouts in a building down the other end (no wooden hall for some Scout groups these days) and perhaps a bowling club, an old people's home and an institute for needy children in between. Result - no park.

Let the Minister for Lands and local councils decide here and now that no more buildings for sectional interests go up on any of our playing-fields or parklands so we may have them for our grandchildren.

Comment. It appears to me the scouts and guides and brownies and cubs are not nearly as numerous in 2017 as they were 50 years ago. I can remember back then that it was hard to get a nap on a Sunday afternoon because of visits from these eager beavers wanting to do odd jobs, or selling cookies, or washing cars.

As an aside, I mention that getting a nap was a foolish dream in any case, given that Mr Whippy and his Greensleeves would come about 3pm, and the lawnmowers on either side would tidy up for the Sunday barbie.

But back to scouts and brownies. I wonder whether their numbers have dropped because there is so much other stuff to do? Or is it that computer games have sapped the energy of the young? Or is there a change in values that say the regimentation into uniforms is no longer acceptable, and even that activities once favoured by scouts are no longer acceptable?

What do you think?

THE *JEPARIT* CAN SAIL

The Federal Government worked out a deal that allows the two strike-bound vessels to sail to Vietnam. For example, on the *Jeparit*, the Seamen's Union had 18 members in the crew, but there were 20 members of other Unions there also. These latter members had no objection to sailing, and so the Government replaced the striking seamen with Navy personnel and the ship went off happily to the war zone.

The extra wages earned by the Navy men, who will still receive their normal pay, will be paid into the RAN Trust Fund, that provides amenities and loans for all Navy personnel.

LITTERBUGGERS

In 1967, this fair nation was hosting a large number of tourists and we were **starting to realise that tourism could be a good source of income and employment.** We still had a very long way to go before we truly exploited this, but the penny was starting to drop. Well, not the full penny, but about the halfpenny would be nearer the mark.

Still, we becoming more conscious of the comments of our visitors. In general, they liked the laid-back people they met, they liked our beaches, and our vast country, and . they liked our politics and our acceptance of democracy.

But some things really turned them off. They hated the accommodation in our pubs, the drinking in our pubs, and the service in our pubs. They laughed at our public transport, our roads, and our accent. But they all commented on how **much litter was to be found** in our streets, our trains, and our beaches, and in any place that we lived or visited.

Letters, J Ferguson, Royal National Park Trust.

The Royal National Part Trust supports very strongly the executive of the Local Government Association of NSW in the proposal seeking power to impose **on-the-spot fines** for litterbugs, and suggests that such power be extended to park authorities.

Strong enforcement of heavy on-the-spot fines is an immediate and tangible means of curbing a rapidly growing social menace. Experiences in the United States, Hong Kong and other places prove the worth of heavy fines and gaol sentences.

The decision of the Local Government Association to ask the Education Department to launch a special campaign to foster tidiness among students also is a good one. But why not go further and **have included in the curriculum** of both primary and secondary schools appropriate courses in hygiene and social behaviour with special emphasis on mental and physical tidiness? This would inculcate an early and lasting understanding of the need for social disciplines.

With an area of 40,000 acres and an annual influx of 1,500,000 visitors, the trust is confronted with extreme problems. Almost the complete workforce is now fully occupied in cleaning up after each weekend in preparation for the next. Following a recent weekend, 1,000 empty bottles were collected within the relatively small area known as Wattamolla.

Indifferent adults, reckless youth, motor cars, iceboxes, modern packaging, non-returnable bottles and cans are helping to develop a truly "effluent" society, and unless present trends are severely curbed, many otherwise pleasant and attractive places will be avoided rather than patronised by normal people.

The Royal National Park Trust is currently considering: a survey of existing facilities for the depositing of rubbish, and seeing to it that proper use is made of such facilities; polite and appropriate advice to be given patrons on entering the park; increased supervision by regular and honorary rangers; prosecution in respect of any offence; the strongest possible case to be made out against offenders; and, failing improvement, park work and supervision force to be increased and extra costs, failing Government grant, to be met from increased parking and service charges.

AN ODD PIECE ABOUT BAPTISM

Letters, Margaret Norman. In the "Herald" of March 8, there is a news item from London concerning Anglican changes in Baptism services. The report begins: "The Church of England is planning to bring back candles and the sign of the Cross to Baptism services."

These words are misleading, although under the circumstances the confusion is understandable. The Church of England has never ceased to use the sign of the Cross at Baptism. Every child is signed with the Cross as directed by the rubric.

I have not read the Archbishop of Canterbury's statement, but believe that the misapprehension arises from his referring to the restoration of the chrism or holy oil with which the child was anointed when signed at Baptism - a practice which was retained in the first Prayer Book of Edward VI (1549) but discontinued in the second (1552). The restoration of this ceremony at adult Baptism and at Confirmation (if allowed by the canons) is included in the proposed revised services for Australia.

Comment. This little piece reminds me that the world about us was becoming **more secular**, and the influence of the churches was definitely falling. Though, **many of its important rituals were still in place.** Most people were baptised, they flocked to the churches for their wedding, and some of the churches had sacraments for the dying and dead, and for Confirmation. The major rituals were still there, and many were almost universally patronised.

This apparent contradiction - falling attendances versus widespread usage - is puzzling. **Perhaps** the explanation lies in the fact that weddings and baptisms were **social** ceremonies, that required **no religious commitment or interest at all**. But Sunday church services were not like that, and any one who went along did so for the religious component. Put it this way, **marriages could still achieve their purpose if God suddenly went away. But Sunday Mass would be worthless without God. The concept of God was no longer a best seller.**

Once again, I ask your opinion.

WHAT WAS A DALLEY?

This Letter appeared under the above heading.

Letters, H Gibbney. I am editing for publication the memoirs of a New South Wales prospector on the Western Australian goldfields in the 1890s.

At one stage, when describing how a lucky prospector was undecided whether to sell his mine or develop it himself, he says: "The only equipment he had with which to develop it was a few shovels, a pick and Dalley the little worker."

The phrase "Dalley the little worker" does not appear in any of the Australian slang dictionaries that I have consulted and after searching for some time, I am inclined to think that the meaning will only emerge from the memory of an old-timer.

If any of your older readers can help, I would be grateful if they would write to me at the Research School of Social Sciences, Australian National University, Canberra.

Letters, H Howe. I agree that the "Dalley" mentioned by Mr H Gibbney was actually a "dolley" or "dolly."

I spent some years at school around Coolgardie and Kalgoorlie in the late 1890s and early 1900s, and worked there later on. I have never heard of a "Dalley" in connection with any prospecting equipment.

As Mr B Bell said, the dolly was a stout iron or steel pot - a mortar - in which quartz could be crushed to fine sand to facilitate the extraction of any gold content.

Dollies were only used for crushing "specimen" ore - that is, ore in which gold was freely visible. As it took the best part of an hour's work to "dolly" a couple of pounds weight of ore, it will be obvious that only rich ore was worth processing. Prospectors habitually dollied their specimen ore and sent poorer grade stone to the nearest battery for crushing. If their claims were for sale, however, they usually dropped a few lumps of specimen stone in with the bulk sent to the battery.

In WA mines, the miners occasionally came across patches of specimen ore, and as their creed was "finding's keeping," it was usually smuggled out of the mine to be dollied at home after work. On rare occasions they broke into a "jeweler's shop" where gold showed freely over a fair expanse of ore - sometimes right across the face being worked. I remember such a "jeweler's shop" where the gang at the face estimated over 1,000 ounces of gold were showing. The immediate problem on all such finds was, of course, to get the gold out of the mine before the management heard about it.

From the time the mines were first opened until the late 1920s, mine managements considered gold-stealing one of their major problems. The WA Government formed a special detective squad to deal with it. The miners took a different view, regarding any gold they found as their own, and a conviction for gold-stealing as just a bit of hard luck and no stain on a man's character.

Most schoolkids on the goldfields considered dollying ore that the old man brought home from work as one of the regular after-school household chores. When not in use, the dolly and pestle were buried in the backyard or adjacent bush, out of sight of inquisitive detectives of the gold-stealing squad.

The phrase "Dalley the little worker" used by Mr Gibbney is quite unknown to me. The nearest to it I remember is the invariably enthusiastic and untruthful prospectors' reports on every new claim pegged - always described in the nearest pub as "good enough to work with a dolly."

Letters, H Gibbney. I express my thanks to the astonishing number of readers who have been kind enough to try to help me solve the problem presented by the phrase "Dalley the little worker." They suggest, without exception, that the word "Dalley" in the text is a corruption of "dolley." When I wrote my original letter I thought otherwise, but I am now convinced.

FENCES ARE DIVISIVE

The Principal of the North Sydney Boys High School was plagued by a wall that was slowly falling down, and a shortage of funds. He thought that as a learning experience he could get his students to patch the wall, and make it safe. The boys did that with gusto.

However, the Principal was strongly criticised for organising this by people who said this was taking away the work that should have gone to tradesmen of the Building Workers Industrial Union. Letters take up the story.

Letters, S Lewis, NSW Teachers' Federation. During the course of their work in a year, teachers are called on to perform a great variety of duties - duties which would otherwise be carried out by clerks, nursing and first-aid attendants, milk distributors, laboratory assistants and workshop attendants, bus conductors, repair and maintenance workers, garbage collectors, patrol officers. Representatives of the NSW Teachers' Federation will be happy to discuss with representatives of the appropriate unions and professional associations the taking over of these duties by people other than teachers. So far our success in this direction with the authorities has been very limited.

Letters, (Mrs) L McCarthy.

My husband, who is a bricklayer, has been having great difficulty in finding work and many of his friends have been out of work for weeks because of the slump in the building industry.

Mr Crawford complained that no local tradesmen were available at short notice to do the work. If he had advertised, or if he had simply answered an advertisement from bricklayers looking for work, he would have been inundated with replies and could have had an immediate start made on the wall.

Although I'm not generally a supporter of the BWIU, I think it is quite right in calling attention to these activities, instigated by a member of a profession which enjoys more protection than any other I can call to mind.

Letters, (Mrs) R Roberts. My congratulations to the headmaster of North Sydney Boys' High School for his leadership in getting his pupils to exercise initiative and economy in bricklaying for a much-needed retaining wall. My two sons did not go to his school, but, oh, how I wish they had!

APRIL NEWS ITEMS

Guess who's here for a seven-concert tour. The famed **Herb Alpert, with his Tijuana Brass**. Last year he had three of the top four best-selling American albums for **his bull-ring style music.**

Protestant clergyman, **Ted Knoff, of Sydney's Wayside Chappel** warned that teenagers were in danger of falling into **a new cult whose members are known as "hippies...."**

Members take **a new drug called LSD, or acid,** and as a result, they experience vivid hallucinations **on "trips" that last up to 12 hours....**

The cult has its origins in America, and Knoff has discovered that it has been in operation there for two years, and that members appear to lose any concern for their personal appearance. He is concerned that the drug can cause brain damage or even death, but **is hopeful that it will not gain a foothold in Australia.**

The **new TABs** across the nation are beset by a **new problem. Gunmen are walking into empty agencies and demanding cash at gun-point.** This week a manageress of a TAB in Melbourne was **shot and killed,** after refusing to open a safe....

The Victorian Police Commissioner said that **it was inevitable** that such killings would occur. A reward of 10,000 Pounds has been offered, by the State Government, for information leading to a conviction.

The Minister for the Army said that at the moment about **one quarter of the troops in active service are**

National Servicemen. In the future, **this will be raised to 50 per cent....**

There will be many families and girl-friends who will not be anxious to see the **babies moved to the front line.**

Graziers near Cobar in the north-west of NSW are having **trouble with eaglehawks** which dive-bomb in packs of 25, and have a wing-span of nine feet. **Lambs are the current target**, because the drought had wiped out young kangaroos. One farmer has **lost 600 lambs in the last three months....**

An employee of the Pastures Protection Board told how 30 eagles had **dive-bombed a horse,** and frightened it so much that it had run into a fence and stunned itself. **The eagles then ripped it to shreds and feasted on its carcase.**

Australian Catholic Bishops have **removed the ban that forbade Catholics from eating meat on Fridays.** The ban will still hold for the Fridays of Lent. It suggested that the faithful **could** instead, on Fridays, make a donation to charity, or abstain from alcohol, smoking, luxury goods and entertainment....

They did not dwell on the fate of millions of dead who had been **consigned to Hell for the mortal sin of eating meat on Friday. Would they be released and go to a better place?** And **they** did **not** elaborate on whether the ban was still relaxed if Catholics went overseas. Would all Catholics **world-wide** be free to eat a pie when they wanted it?

JUMPING HORSES

The racing calendar in Australia was set by various State bodies, and a few of these contained races known as Hurdles and Steeples. These were very long-distance races with perhaps twenty or more hurdles of brushwood placed across the track, with the racing horses required to jump them In some cases, a water hazard was placed on the far side of the jump, so that any horse that cleared the hurdle had also to get enough distance to clear the water as well. Failure to do either resulted in the horse falling, and the jockey being thrown. Often, half the horses crashed, and did not finish.

After the war, Victoria was the only State that kept these races in its regular calendar. Two hurdle races per week at major tracks were allowed, and these generally were the first and third race on the programme. Betting on them was enthusiastic, even though there was no way of guessing who would finish, never mind the best horse.

In Britain, such races were on their calendar as well, and the **Grand National Steeplechase** was the premier such event. In 1967, 44 horses started. One riderless horse blocked six riders near the 23rd hurdle, and these got tangled. The rest of the field crashed into them or the hurdle, and only Foinavon got over in the first try. Eight of the fallen jockeys re-mounted and went back and successfully jumped the hurdle, and finished hundreds of yards behind Foinavon.

The crashes were heard right round the racing world. They gave a great impetus to **the animal right advocates who said that such races were cruel**. Almost all race tracks, here and abroad, gradually restricted the number of

Hurdles and Steeples on the annual calendar. So much so, it became hard to find them on a regular basis, other than in annual National events.

MORE CURES FOR DELINQUENCY

Our teeny-boppers and teens were still causing havoc, and of course there were dozens of suggestions for fixing or controlling the little darlings.

The Letter below has its own ideas, and the first half raises an issue that was well ahead of its times.

Letters, Shirley Humphrey. Everybody is running around in circles, searching for a reason for the wave of violence and irresponsibility among young people. Experts are consulted and their words are read closely by the public. But not anywhere in all this verbiage does one find mentioned the fact that many young, and not so young, people are not only undernourished but often in an extreme state of malnutrition.

Some people blame working mothers for the deeds of their offspring, because they go to work, NEVER because they often perhaps do not see to it that the family is properly fed.

Research is carried out in many fields. Let there be a Government investigation into the state of health of all persons, especially the young, who are troublesome. Find out if they eat the essentials for good health such as cheese, salad greens, milk, meat, eggs, etc. Then it will be easy to see if the parents are to blame. If the body is not healthy, then neither is the brain, which could very well be the reason for the hooliganism, with a very much darker state of affairs ahead.

Young people can be seen everywhere, at midday, eating something greasy out of paper bags. Good nutrition is not considered because the modern cult is one of emaciation, and so they don't care whether they eat or not.

Drug-taking must be another cause of bad nutrition. The young person, perhaps a student, finds that he cannot concentrate, goes to a doctor for "something," instead of trying to correct his diet, and progresses gradually to stronger and more harmful drugs, which further prevent his wish for good food.

Our Government should try to instill a sense of responsibility into our young people, to take good care of their health, because they, after all, are the future of this country.

Comment. The second part of the Letter relating to drug-taking of course has a lot of relevance today when malnourished druggies can be seen everywhere. Back in the early days of drugs, the link was not so apparent.

But, in a world that seemed full of children, the problems they were "responsible" for kept popping up. Letter-writers told us that they, travelling in trains in bunches, clogged the aisles, took all the seats, were rude and noisy, opened or shut doors or windows, vomited out the doors, piddled while passing through stations, and put feathers up the nostrils of a sleeping drunk.

One of their minor faults was discussed here.

Letters, (Mrs) S Clarke. There have been several letters recently, discussing whether or not children should remain seated in trains while adults stand. Apart from the obvious reason of age versus youth, I feel that as schoolchildren pay little or no fares at all, this is justification enough for them vacating seats for adults, who pay quite a considerable sum for the privilege of travelling on trains.

If the children wish to remain seated, then it is only fair that they be charged full adult fares. Notices could be posted in trains to this effect, with the offending children being reported and their parents billed for the extra amount.

VIETNAM NEWS

The battles in Vietnam were still raging. Napalm bombs were being dropped more frequently. They were now being used to defoliate large areas of jungle, so that heavy-bombers could better target enemy forces. Large numbers of citizens were being burned to death as a result.

The Letter below was one of the first decrying this development. As this weapon was gradually used more and more by the Americans, the trickle of Letters swelled to a tide.

Letters, Dawn Gietzelt. In the January issue of "Redbook," Dr Richard Perry, a volunteer physician in South Vietnam three times in three years, writes that "The Vietcong do not use napalm; we do... I have been an orthopedic surgeon for a good number of years, with a rather wide range of medical experience. But nothing could have prepared me for my encounters with Vietnamese women and children burned by napalm. It was shocking and sickening, even for a physician, to see and smell the blackened flesh..."

And Martha Gellhorn in the January issue of the "Ladies' Home Journal" reports: "Before I went to Saigon, I had heard and read that napalm melts the flesh, and I thought that's nonsense, because I can put a roast in the oven and the fat will melt but the meat stays there. Well, I went and saw these children burned by napalm, and it is absolutely true. The chemical reaction of this napalm does melt the flesh and the flesh runs down their faces on to their chests and it sits there and it grows there..."

The International Committee of the Red Cross reported that there are 30,000 known child victims of napalm. There are undoubtedly many, many more whose tragedy is not known.

Mr Robert McNamara has been quoted (I F Stone's Weekly, February 2) as saying that in the fiscal year 1967-68, $31m will be spent for napalm. Are we supposed to believe that the US is manufacturing this colossal amount of napalm, but not using it? A UNESCO population study in 1964 gives 47.5 per cent of the Vietnamese as being under 16 years. How many children are among the casualties?

I am appalled and ashamed that Australians, in supporting the US in Vietnam, are condoning the use of such a monstrous and barbaric weapon against backward peasants and little children. Irrespective of our views on Vietnam, let us all urge the Federal Government to use its influence with the US to stop the use of napalm!

THE HORRORS OF RODEO

Once a year, every country district had a rodeo come to the local showground. There were always many horses that came with the troupe, and a few excellent riders. A **main attraction was the buckjumping.** The idea was that a rider should get on a horse, and a loin rope would excite the horse, and start it bucking, and the rider would stay aboard for as long as possible. Local lads and horses were encouraged to enter, and the hospitals would be warned in advance that quite a few concussions would be coming their way.

At this time, there was almost no resistance from the animal rights communities that developed in later years. Still, in the second Letter below, the matter of animal cruelty was to the fore, and heralded the concern that grew to the stage now when the rodeo industry is closely regulated and always on the defensive.

Letters, Jack Walsh. R Bullock's letter had me   in hysterics.

Mr Bullock's version of the **rib-tickling flank strap** on the buckjumpers certainly takes the equestrian cake; this learned gentleman states that the flank strap **tickles** the horse, thus making it buck savagely, and that any horse grabbed by the flank will lash out! Doesn't Mr Bullock know that the essence of good training is in teaching a horse to be handled all over? I would consider it gross bad manners and poor training if my own horses lashed out if grabbed by the flanks or any other part of the body for that matter.

Now, let's get down to a few truths about the pros and cons of rodeo cruelty. Although not physically cruel, making horses buck by putting a flank strap on them **is a form of mental torture**. The flank strap is fastened around the horse in an unnatural position. It is annoying, upsets the horse's sense of balance and equilibrium, and is without doubt responsible for instilling in the horse fear from which it tries to escape by bucking and contorting its body in an effort to remove the flank strap. Try tying a handkerchief lightly round a domestic cat in the same position as a flank strap - the cat will have the greatest difficulty in walking and will repeatedly fall down. Buckjumpers are undoubtedly fear-crazed and I consider it to be moronic and cruel to permit promoters to make money out of the discomfort of terror-stricken animals.

Mr Bullock states that Rocky Ned, Dargan's Grey, Firefly and Warrigal lived to a great old age. Of course they did - the promoters are not going to kill the goose that lays the golden egg! What about the poor animals that don't make the grade, and only contest second-class rodeos? They are frequently poorly fed, subjected to cruelty and physical abuse by their handlers and invariably finish up as dogs' meat. On Wednesday, March 22, at the rodeo session at the Sydney Royal Easter Show, patrons were subjected to the horrifying sight of two buckjumpers careering around the ring fear-crazed and crashing head-on. One horse was killed outright - not my idea of fun.

No, this is not a ticklish affair. It is without a shadow of doubt cruelty.

Comment. A Mr Burke from Cessnock followed up with a note that mentioned the plight of the horses on merry-go-rounds. He pointed out that they stood still in the open for days on end, and went round and round, and many of the riders were untrained and thus quite rough. He pleaded that, while they had to earn their keep, they should be released on Mondays and Tuesdays to enjoy some pasture-time.

I find it hard to argue against this.

SELF INDULGENCE

Occasionally, about once a book, I have a few moments when I let myself roam all over the page, with nothing much in mind. Right now I am about to do this.

Christianity, and most other religions, is based on the concept of **each person having a soul** that is immortal and will persist after the death of that person. It is an elusive concept, and different Christian religions have their own take on what it is and how important it is.

In 1967, there was a considerable interest in some circles in arguing the finer points of theology. This went way beyond the Bible episodes that clergy pushed out in monotonous Sunday sermons, and went well into the realms of philosophy and ethics as well.

I enclose a Letter that touched on some of this. I suggest you just skim it at first, and then go to my Comment below.

Letters, (Rev) Brian Heawood. Professor Lloyd Geering asserts that "man has no immortal soul", and Dr Alan Loy supports him in an article entitled "Do we have immortal souls?". Surely the real question at issue is "Are we immortal souls?" Professor Geering and Dr Loy say we are not, and both draw a distinction between immortality and resurrection. Is that distinction valid?

Both claim that life-after-death is the gift of God and that there is no such thing as natural immortality. But is not life-before-death equally the gift of God? It is no more "natural" than life-after-death, Christians see all life as God's gift. Of course, God "raises" us into life-after-death; we might say with equal truth that He "raises" us into life-before-death. Surely both states of existence are equally "natural" and equally "the gift of God"?

Surely the traditional (and biblical) view is that man is a soul made by God in His own image, and that he has a physical body for use in this life and will have a "spiritual body" for use in the life to come, both physical and spiritual bodies being God's gift. If God is the source of all life, physical and spiritual, the distinction between immortality and resurrection seems meaningless. God has made all men; obviously mortality is the lot of all men; but in Jesus Christ God "has broken the power of death and brought life and immortality to light through the Gospel" (II Timothy 1:9-10).

Comment. I suggested that you just skim-read this Letter because it is not possible for an untrained reader to understand all the nuances of the Letter. I gave it to you just as an example, one of many, of **the type of discussions that were much more common then than they are now, 50 years later.**

In the media world of 2017, it is **very hard to find any sort of philosophical or religious debate.** Today it is all gotcha politics, divorcing celebrities, and tear-jerking sob stories. Any Letters published are angry, contemptuous, and superior and selfish.

As I read the above Letter, and looked at today's efforts, I had a burst of nostalgia for the good old days of yesteryear. How I would like to have an old-fashioned argument with some opponents who would listen longer than 30 seconds, and themselves be able to argue at least three sides to any question.

But let me finish my meander. I note with nostalgia **that Debating Societies have almost disappeared.** All large suburbs, and all country cities had one of these, and it met about once a fortnight. Perhaps three women would argue that "Women need religion more than men", and three men might argue that it was men who were most in need.

Whatever the topic, **the debate was strictly controlled.** No interruptions, lots of effusive courtesy, hand-shaking at the end. Each speaker presented in about eight minutes, then there were rebuttals, and sometimes rebuttals of rebuttals. All very civilised, and the whole show, including a cuppa in the middle, took two or more hours.

Alas, my friends, all gone.

In any case, my moment of self-indulgence has passed.
It could be that tomorrow I will look at what I have just
written, and decide to junk it. In that case, there will be a
space here. So, if you see such a space, you will know what
happened.

NEWS AND VIEWS

Letters, Kerwin Maegraith. What a disgraceful state
of affairs when Scotland, representing the greatest of
all, and the only truly international game of football,
Soccer, can be deprived of our only suitable ground
to hold a Test match - the Sydney Cricket Ground.
This is typical of the silly provincialism of Sydney, the
only capital in the world where the wonders of Rugby
League are written about so profusely, generally to the
detriment of the other games of football.

When footballers come here who have global prominence
in publicity, they are relegated to the backblocks of the
Showground, suitable for exhibiting prize bulls but not
world-renowned footballers. Doesn't Australia want
world publicity?

As an Australian, I lived in Britain long enough to
watch Soccer executives many a time help out their
poor Rubgy League cousins in the north (where this
offshoot of Rugby is indulged in), by providing their best
grounds for "Test matches," but evidently the hill-billy
mind of the locals here does not understand the value of
such an epic visit as Scotland or, later on, Manchester
United. Other countries would jump in the air to get
such stars, but I suppose we are expected to watch
Denis Law and the like through a telescope through
the folly of antipodean small minds and parish pump
politics in sport. Can Mr Askin get the intelligentsia to
change their minds?

MAY NEWS ITEMS

A **referendum was held in NSW** on the matter of **creating a new State in the north-west of the state**. The matter had been debated for a long time, with supporters from the Tamworth region particularly vocal. However, the poll showed that **the State overall was against the idea**, and NO votes totalled 200,000 while the YES camp got 170,000.

Andrew Jones was a young man, **only 22 years of age, who was elected to Federal Parliament** by his electorate of Adelaide. He was an ultra-conservative, and at the time was the youngest person to be elected to the House. He loved the limelight....

But not at this time. At a Liberal Club dinner in his home city, he claimed in an after-dinner speech that some **Members of Parliament were half drunk half the time.....**

He went on to say that he had been disillusioned by the "**filth, smut, jealousy and friction**" of politics in Canberra. He described alcohol as "devil's urine"....

As a result of the speech, **Mr Jones was not popular with his colleagues**, and he was forced to withdraw his statements, much to his distress. He was not all that popular at the next elections either when he **lost his seat with a 14 per cent swing against him**.

Sir Francis Chichester was about to end his **lone round-the-world sailing epic** in a small yacht. This journey had brought him to Sydney. In passing, he had been knighted en route, **he had received massive media**

coverage at every stage, and he was expected to be back in Plymouth in a few days....

That fair English city, though, decided that **he should not be made a "freeman"** which would have given him the Freedom of the City....

The local Council remembered that this honour had always been made to **persons who had given 50 years service to the City**. Despite "drawing the attention of the world to Plymouth", he was not granted the privilege.

Britain has applied to join the European Common Market. That means Australia and the Empire will no longer be given preferences in trade matters, and will be competing against European countries in equal terms. This had been mooted for years, but **the reality of it gave this Australia a nasty shock**....

Jumping 50 years ahead, to 2017, the Brits have just elected to **leave the Common Market. Brexit, though, will not stir up the same consternation as Brentry did.**

A Teachers College at Sydney's Paddington, run by the NSW Education Department, has banned the wearing of shorts, slacks and jeans. The reason is that the students there should learn to dress in a manner appropriate for the classroom after they graduate. Students will protest.

At Bendigo, **a TAB agency was robbed** of $2,000 by three hooded men at gun-point. There was nothing really unusual about this. What **was** noteworthy was that **the next morning, three policemen were charged with the offence.**

FOOT AND MOUTH DISEASE

When **foot and mouth disease** gets a foothold in a country, it means that **herds of animals must be killed** and their **carcases burnt**. There was concern that, if the disease spread to Australia from Britain, then our marsupials might also need to be destroyed. Over the last two years, tests have proved that **the disease will not spread among our marsupials** and other animals.....

To prove this, red kangaroos, tree kangaroos, Bennett's wallabies, wombats, possums, bandicoots, marsupial mice, echidnas and water rats have been flown to England and tested. They did not spread the disease among themselves or among cattle....

Comment. What a disaster it might have been if they had been found to be carriers.

THE YANKS ARE COMING

A writer voiced his opinion on US troops visiting here on Rest and Recreation leave.

Letters, Andrew Rosinski. I hope the Federal Government has enough wisdom and enough say in the matter **to reject any request from the US Government to send troops from Vietnam here** for recuperation. This is not the first time the US Government has attempted to do this. Several months ago attempts were made to "sound out" public reaction on the Gold Coast residents, but they were unsuccessful; the residents objected.

I do not think that the presence of large numbers of foreign troops, even though they are our allies, will benefit our city or the Gold Coast or Brisbane. Soldiers, although they are only men in uniforms, behave differently from the rest of the population. Their uniforms give them some anonymity - more freedom and licence to do things they would not dream of doing if they were in civilian life. Even if they wore civilian clothes on leave, these men would look for the light type of entertainment which I hope will not spread far beyond King's Cross. It would increase the number of "ladies of commerce" in that area and, I feel sure, bring more problems to the hard-working police there. For this type of leave, Hong Kong, Tokyo or Bangkok, I feel, are more suitable than Sydney.

The American soldiers take their leave also in Hawaii, which is a State of their own country, and where life is quite pleasant, so why look for other places? Some people may point out the financial advantages from an increased number of these "tourists," which would bring some foreign exchange to the hard-pressed exchequer. I feel that the disadvantages would outweigh the advantages and we do not need dollars that badly.

News Item. No one took any notice of this plea, and the US Army **said it** will send 12,000 soldiers per month to take Rest and Recreation leave in Sydney, Brisbane and the Gold Coast.

A number of Letter writers warned that the Yanks were not always well behaved in their last invasion here during WWII, and hoped that this time we will not be so subservient and tolerant. But, **opinions differed.**

Letters, Peter Kelly. Who's this selfish character, Andrew Rosinski, who pontificates that he doesn't think American troops will benefit Sydney, Brisbane or the Gold Coast on their leave from Vietnam?

Isolated, his thought is true enough, as was equally true in Hitler's war that numbers of Australians did little to enhance the respectability of Cairo, Edmonton or London. In their natural pursuit of the pleasures of the flesh (not one whit more earthy but a mite more enjoyable than the hell they're coming to Sydney, etc., to escape), troops never do any place a power of good. And, indeed, they were never yet let loose in any city for the city's good.

But so what? Shameful it might be if the ladies of the night at King's Cross expanded their operation to Mr Rosinski's Turramurra (but surely all business follows opportunity?) and other esteemed centres; nevertheless, most of us with our own memories of war will gladly welcome our heroic visitors as friends, just as we'll equally happily risk the occasional damage they may do or the provocations provided by some of our girls.

Let us remember that these fellows haven't just been risking a spot of damage to their own or anyone else's image… they've been risking their necks.

Letters, (Mrs) E Gray. To bring large numbers of American Servicemen here on leave is undesirable for three reasons. **First**, acceleration of the unfortunate Americanisation of this city; **second**, a recurrence of shortage of taxis and other services to the Australian public; **third**, it is a fact of life that foreign Servicemen in a country, being birds of passage, are a danger to our daughters. The fact that America assisted us in World War II is no reason for eternal permissiveness as regards American activity here. The place for Americans on leave is America - with their own wives and sweethearts.

Letters, F Skinner. Surely Andrew Rosinski is joking when he objects to US troops being on leave in Australia. I have not read such drivel in years.

Soldiers do behave differently from the vast mass of the population. If the crime statistics for a similar number of soldiers and civilians were examined he would not be very impressed with the result. At one stage I served over 14 years with one battalion and during this period there was only one "serious" Court-martial and the charge was "stealing"! A soldier does not hide behind his uniform with anonymity. He wears it with pride and is proud of its association with tradition and manhood.

It might prove interesting to know what percentage of the earnings of the ladies of the King's Cross area comes from the Forces compared with civilians. To suggest that gratification of one's lust is easier in Eastern countries is balderdash. In all, I served some 35 years and spent over 13 in Eastern countries and, to give only one example, I would not hesitate to say that in Singapore (which has a population similar to metropolitan Sydney) that there are far fewer prostitutes.

As a matter of interest, I have read the US Military Penal Code. Included under sexual offences are fornication and adultery (not offences in British law) and the maximum punishment is very high.

If the brutal and licentious soldiery did not exist, Mr Rosinski might well look forward to being employed as a coolie by the Chinese.

Letters, Michael Marsh, American ex-Serviceman. These men are mostly conscripts. Thus they represent a cross-section, socially and morally, of America. They are not libidinous criminals who will all gravitate to the Cross and the Gold Coast. I have lived in Australia for six years, and I can assure you that social and moral attitudes are extremely similar in our two countries. With respect to the "birds of passage" and "danger to our daughters" attitude of Mrs E Gray, I suggest that our daughters (I have two) will get what they ask for, and that this will depend on their upbringing.

With regard to the Americanisation of Australia: this is being accomplished mostly in the wrong sort of way, via television and advertising, that is, along a one-way channel of communication. Giving a few thousand, or maybe tens of thousands of Americans, a week's taste of Australia may be the most effective possible way of Australianising America. Are you afraid that you have no culture to export? I can assure you that you have.

The businesses that will be benefited by these visitors will chiefly be the transport and hotel industries. The troops will be found at the Alice, on the slopes of Mt Kosciusko, and up at the Lamington Plateau. And if Australians continue to be their friendly, generous selves, then these troops will have gained something positive from their period of war service.

One last plea - for heaven's sake, let's not dump 10,000 American troops on about 5,000 unsuspecting native Gold Coasters. Much better for all to dilute them in Sydney!

BABY BONUS?

Australia had just lived through a baby boom and was now starting to get an echo of that as the early boomers themselves begot their own ankle biters. Still, in terms of the world's population, we were a small, almost trifling, nation. This gave us much freedom for the adventurous acts of wild colonial boys and girls in many ways, but it left us exposed to the threats that we could see as the nations around us grew more and more independent and nationalistic. It turned out that they posed no threat to us at all, but at the time the cry of "populate or perish" was heard everywhere in the Halls of Power.

But were the authorities that pushed that line really serious? Granted we had imported a million migrants since the war, and we had retained a high percentage of these. This was no mean feat. But what social measures had we employed?

Letters, A Keston. It was a pleasure to read recent discussions in the "Herald" and the "Financial Review" regarding child endowment and its association with the falling birthrate.

I am sure that if **child endowment was increased**, the average family would think in terms of more than one or two children. After all, endowment means the "provision of permanent means of support." And in Australia that means 50 cents a week a child. What is 50 cents today? What can one buy for 50 cents? How much does a mother spend weekly for a baby or child?

France, after a history of falling birthrate, managed between 1946 and 1955 to increase the population by nearly three million, between 1955 and 1965 by five million. The reason for this is quoted as being mainly due to the generous assistance the Government gave, in the form of family bonuses, allowances and facilities for medical treatment.

The plea for higher child endowment will only be successful if the matter is kept alive, by both the public and our Press.

The next writer goes a step further. Australian governments, one after the other, were always anxious to provide for the health of the nation. They had adopted over the years many different policies that they hoped would do this. By now, it was accepted that the population would benefit if it set policies so that if **individuals and families took out some health insurance**, then the government would help them to meet hospital and medical costs as they arose. This was a voluntary approach, and left many people outside the safety net. It also did not cover many people who **did** subscribe for many of the more expensive operations and procedures that they would come to need.

At the moment, the policy was a step in the right direction, but it would be true to say that it could be improved mightily. For example, in Britain, there was a **universal** nationalised health system, paid for by taxes, that provided coverage for virtually all maladies.

Letters, C Smith. We read in the daily papers that doctors' fees are to go up again. May one ask where is it all going to end? Has this country become a Mecca for "get-rich-quick-medics" at the expense of the poor and the sick?

As it stands now, those most in need of medical attention are those least able to afford it - wage-earners on low incomes, people with young children with only one income, older people who have not yet reached the pension age. Hospital and medical funds are not the answer because many cannot afford their ever-increasing tariffs either. One payment behind and the family is "unfinancial," a good word to avoid paying out. These are profit-making organisations, no matter how they set themselves up, and under the present system are out to make money at the expense of human suffering.

One of the outstanding causes **why migrants run back home** is because of the complete disregard of their plight in times of sickness. They feel insecure and live in daily fear of becoming ill and having nowhere to turn. Many of them come from countries where this fear is unknown and they have never had to face it. If a young migrant is not in a hospital and medical fund at least 10 months no benefits for maternity can be claimed. Many young women are pregnant when they arrive and have to find the whole cost of their hospitalisation themselves. Is this fair or right?

My family and self have always voted for a Liberal Government. But for the record, our votes in future will go to the party with the courage to come up with a plan for some form of **socialisation of the medical services**, and so will thousands of others, as this measure is long overdue, no matter what fight the AMA may make to keep its members' fat pockets lined.

Comment. So, the woman above has the **British** example in mind when she argues that she wants socialised medicine. And, she suggests, if this were provided, more migrants would stay. There were others who wrote to say that the lack of such had stopped them from migrating in the first place.

All in all, and back to an earlier question, how serious were the authorities in arguing the populate-or-perish line?

NO OIL SPILLS HERE

Australia was new to the oil exploration business. Other nations in the world had over half a century of experience at getting the black gold to the surface, and more recently, were developing off-shore methods as well.

But this was a world where the environment **on a large scale** was not a great concern. Granted, local pressure groups were forming that fumed over the policies of governments that fouled some area in their proximity, but the formation of large-scale groups to protest against national and international despoilage was in its infancy.

Still, there had been murmurings of late against the dangers posed by possible spillage around off-shore oil developments. The gentleman below, with his obvious superior technical knowledge, set our minds at rest.

Letters, J Flower, Petroleum Information Bureau. The fear that offshore oil exploration and production may cause pollution of the sea, expressed by H Inglis, could possibly be widely shared, but fortunately it is almost groundless.

I say "almost" because accidents can happen despite the stringent precautions taken to prevent them. The blowout preventer, a standard piece of control equipment on all drilling rigs, is employed to obviate "gushers." Comprising a series of valves capable of withstanding very high pressures, it is operated hydraulically or pneumatically, with manual operation available in an emergency.

Once an offshore producing well has been completed, its oil flow is controlled and regulated by another series of valves, fitted at the wellhead either on the seabed or on a production platform standing 60 feet or so above water level.

The two principal oil industry standards authorities, the American Petroleum Institute and the Institute of Petroleum, London, have issued detailed codes for the design, construction and operation of offshore drilling, production and transportation equipment, as well as manuals of safe practice to be observed by all concerned.

As a newcomer to offshore oil and gas production, Australia is able to take advantage of the very latest techniques and safety practices developed for this branch of the industry overseas.

There is, of course, a legal obligation on exploration and production companies to conduct their operations safely and to prevent wastage of oil or natural gas.

Comment. Sounds good. But didn't always work.

CHICHESTER'S TRAVEL TIME

In a recent submission, the Editor of the *SMH* found much to praise in the epic round-the-world efforts of Sir Francis Chichester. At one stage, though, he appeared to be about to deprecate the man and his achievement. He said, " He failed to equal the record time set by clipper ships on their way from Plymouth to Sydney. He has widened no horizons and added nothing to our knowledge of the physical world. His journey was accomplished with techniques of radio communication, meteoroligical science, oceanology and marine engineering unknown to the ancient mariners."

The editor though, added that for a frail, bespectacled old man to set forth alone and return home, it was a grand feat that will secure his place in history.

One reader had no problems with the conclusions of the Editor, but he did want to tidy up some sailing facts.

Letters, Graham Bennett. No one can add to or detract from Sir Francis Chichester's magnificent achievement. The record should be set right however on the one point which has been consistently incorrect among all the thousands of words written on the subject. In Tuesday's "Herald," the editorial states that Sir Francis "failed to equal the time of 100 days set by the old clipper ships on their outward journey from Plymouth to Sydney."

In an era of manned rockets, it has become customary to designate as a "clipper" any vessel with even one square sail. Clippers were highly specialised freaks which had their heyday in the 1870s. They were small, fast vessels with very limited cargo capacity built expressly to carry premium cargoes, such as the tea which they carried from China to London.

Clipper time between the United Kingdom and Australia was 60 to 65 days and any clipper captain who took 100 days for the trip would find himself out of a job. The last surviving clipper is the Cutty Sark. By contrast, the big barques which carried the bulk of the world's cargoes at the turn of the century were a much more efficient machine.

Given good weather and a good crew, these efficient cargo vessels could make the UK-Australia trip in 70 to 80 days. So when we speak of 100-day passages over this route, we are referring not to the light, speedy clippers but to the heavy, under-manned cargo vessels of four decades later.

WHITE ENSIGN

Being not at all nautical, I was puzzled by the following Letter.

Letters, James Deane. I express the hope that an opportunity might be found by the naval authorities to show the Australian white ensign to the people.

I know that this ensign can be seen flying from the masts of our naval establishments and our naval vessels; however, from inquiries I have made here and there I find that so far there are few who actually are aware that we now have our own white ensign and fewer still who have seen it.

Each Thursday a ceremony of remembrance is carried out at the Cenotaph, and on occasions the Navy is on parade for this function. On such an occasion, if naval protocol allows, our white ensign could be flown from the flagpole adjacent to the figure representing the Navy on the Cenotaph.

This arrangement would be most effective and would provide the viewing public with an opportunity to appreciate this impressive Australian white ensign.

Comment. I already knew that the ensign was the flag our naval ships sailed under. But I had not realised that the Australian Navy still sailed under the British ensign until the start of the Vietnam war. **Britain never did join into this fray**, yet here we were, fighting in Vietnamese waters, under the flag of the British Navy. So, we changed that and developed our own ensign.

Mind you, we did not change the design all that much. The new ensign is the same as our existing national flag, except that the blue bits became white, and the white bits became blue.

So the above Letter now makes sense to me. I wonder, though, **how long we would have continued with the old one had we not taken a different line from Britain over Vietnam?**

A PENNY A WORD

The British Post Office had for years been proud of its provision to news services of one penny a word for all Press cables to destinations within the Empire. Most Empire nations also offered this cheap rate to other Members of the Commonwealth of nations. This meant that cables could be sent by news organisations from England at a small cost, and this was said to be a contribution that Britain made to the free flow of information to her Empire and throughout the world.

At the moment, Britain was at last formally intent upon joining the European Common Market and was rethinking her links to the Empire.

Letters, E Sommerland. The decision of the British Post Office to abandon the now famous "penny a word" rate for Press cables will be another nail in the coffin of the Commonwealth. This unique concession, applying throughout the Commonwealth, has frequently been quoted as an example to the rest of the world, of enlightened appreciation of the power of news exchanges in creating understanding and co-operation between nations. Trebling the rate will inevitably reduce the flow of information from Britain to the members of the Commonwealth, and if they follow suit, among the Commonwealth nations themselves.

Any such decision should be taken at the highest political level; it is not a matter to be determined by telecommunications administrations on economic grounds. It is said the concession cost the British Post Office a million pounds a year. Surely this was not a high price to pay for such a vital contribution to Commonwealth unity.

Furthermore, the favourable rate was undoubtedly an important factor in establishing London as one of the great telecommunication centres of the world - a status which may not be retained, especially if American traffic is now re-routed.

Australia shares, with the developing countries of the Commonwealth, the disadvantage of being far removed from the new centres of the world. For all of us, more even than for Britain, the two-way flow of information in and out of our countries is vitally important. It keeps us in touch with the rest of the world and projects our image abroad.

Is it too much to hope that the Australian Government will be independent enough and far-sighted enough to preserve the long standing concession so as to encourage the outflow of Australian news, and to use its influence for like action by other Commonwealth countries?

Comment. The writer was correct in judging that Empire bonds were certain to be reduced by such moves.

Second comment. What he did not foresee, **nor did anyone else**, was the immense changes that were to happen in the communications usage over the next half-century.

Probably most readers can remember sending a telegram to someone living in Australia. Sixpence, they cost, for 15 words or less. Then later, they cost a penny a word. How careful we all were in choosing the words that we sent, even locally. If we, rarely, had to communicate overseas, we were even more careful, and for most of us the cost was prohibitive. And all of this meant trips to the Post Office, and perhaps, in the early days, a wait of an hour until the Post Master was ready to work his Morse Code magic. Sending telegrams was deliberate and quite rare.

Look at us now. How many times a day do you use the internet? How much does each visit cost? How much information is sent by everyone to everyone, home and abroad, how many images can travel the world in a single posting?

How quaint it is to talk about a penny a word!

A TOKEN UPDATE ON VIETNAM

The war in Vietnam is still going on, though **I am being careful not to get bogged down with news from there**. Still, I should give you occasional random reminders.

Letters, K Barry. Within 12 months, trained school teachers will be on active service in Vietnam as privates in the infantry. At least one civil engineer that we know of will also serve as a gunner in the artillery.

One would think that the Chinese were already in Darwin. How can the Government excuse this deplorable waste of education and skills?

Soldiers of the Regular Army who have joined up to see active service are equally frustrated. While National Servicemen fill the ranks, the professional soldier misses out on his share of experience in his own sphere.

What is actually being achieved by the Army's extraordinary system of postings?

Letters, James McRorie. The "Herald's" editorial stated that "**it seems to have been demonstrated that bombing is not effective in halting, or even diminishing, the flow of supplies and reinforcement from North to South Vietnam.**"

It is hard to accept such a statement. The hundreds of thousands of bombs the Americans are pouring on to the bases and supply lines of North Vietnam must be hampering very considerably the movement of troops and supplies.

The question is how big would this movement be were it not kept in check by the American bombing. A softer line by the Yanks would probably result in thousands more casualties among the Americans and their allies.

Half-measures will not win battles and timidity never got any country anywhere in any war. As far as Asians are concerned it would be taken as a sign of weakness.

It is becoming clear that **the Yanks are not going to allow themselves to be pinned down to a war of attrition that could last indefinitely** and, understandably smarting under the criticism coming from the sidelines, they are likely to launch at any time an effort that will overshadow anything that has yet taken place in Vietnam.

The pity of it all is that should America bring the present struggle in Vietnam to a successful conclusion, China, unless she tangles with the Soviet Union, will see to it that there is still plenty of trouble in South-East Asia.

Whichever way we look at it there is plenty for us to worry about in the future and the only country from whom we could expect help is our present ally, the United States; and if we want that help it is up to us, whether we are right or wrong, whether we like it or not, to be, in the words of the Prime Minister, "**all the way with LBJ.**"

Letters, Bruce Ashby. The "Herald" editorial "Value of bombing" is unduly optimistic, not to say naive, when it states that "**it is inconceivable that the order for an all-out air assault on North Vietnam should be given.**"

Experience teaches that what is inconceivable today is quite likely to be accepted as a reasonable level of activity tomorrow.

I contend that **there is no limit** that the US will set. The US will go on bombing, and increase the severity until they win or see no point to it. They have no concern for any person on the ground, or for property and infrastructure destroyed.

As the situation worsens, they will drop bigger and better bombs. What we in Australia must do is ask ourselves **whether we will continue to support this**, and how far can it go on before we say that we no longer support the US.

JUNE NEWS ITEMS

The Snowy Mountains Authority has just about done its job of constructing dams and providing irrigation in south-east Australia. This mammoth task has being ongoing for 20 years, and has employed thousands of persons, many of them migrants....

The present workforce will be cut from 3,200 to 700 men who will be used **to do** maintenance.

The Child Welfare Advisory Committee, a body set up by the NSW Government, has suggested that **sex education be taught in primary schools**. Also, that preparatory **courses for marriage and parenthood** be **taught in secondary schools**. Further, these lucky children should also get education in **contraceptive techniques**.

Comment. I expect that there will be some dissent on this. Watch this space.

Our Prime Minister Harold Holt and his wife, Zara, were given **a most lavish dinner** last night by President Johnson at the White House. Johnson gave Holt a speargun, engraved with his initials, as a present. Several hundred guests attended the dinner, and **one highlight** was the appearance midway of a dozen violinists who played *Waltzing Matilda*, and variations on *Tie Me Kangaroo Down Sport*....

A second highlight was the naming of a green and white ice cream dessert topped with cream. In future, Mrs Johnson announced, **this concoction was to be called** *Glace Zara*.

At Waterloo, a suburb of Sydney, a youth threw a cracker into the dray of an open cart. The horse bolted, and the driver was thrown but not badly hurt. The horse carried on, and crashed into a wall, and broke a leg. It had to be shot....

Opposition to *Cracker Night* had been growing for years. On the Empire Day night, hundreds of children and a few adults had annually **ended up in hospitals as a result of burns from exploding fireworks**....

To stop this, this year in Sydney various authorities arranged fireworks displays at local sports grounds where rockets and whiz-bangers could delight the viewing public. It was hoped that this would take the **bonfires out of thousands of streets** and put them into a safer location....

As it turned out, this idea was a good one. Over the years, it has achieved its purpose. Later versions **on News Years Eve** have been enormously successful all round Australia.

Heavy fighting has broken out between Israel and the Arab States. All of this passed **almost unnoticed in insular Australia** as we clustered for the Sunday barbie, thousand of miles from the action....

Except for the occasional liner passenger to Britain. Shipping traffic through the Suez Canal has been stopped because someone or other **bombed a ship as it passed through, and it sank, thereby blocking the Canal for a month.** How it will affect travel is uncertain at the moment.

THE *VOYAGER* AGAIN

Three years ago, the Australian aircraft carrier *Melbourne* cut one of our destroyers, the *Voyager*, into two halves in manoeuvers at Jervis Bay, on the NSW South Coast. This tragedy saw 82 men killed, and many injured. A Royal Commission was held a few months later, and its decision was that the *Melbourne* was responsible for the collision.

Now, a few Federal Parliamentarians were questioning that decision. They were claiming that the Captain of the *Voyager* was intoxicated at the time of the collision, and that the disaster could have been avoided if he had acted differently.

So far, the Government has made the decision to re-open the enquiry, and details will be released soon. It did not finish its report until 1968.

MIXED FORTUNES FOR BIG CELEBRITIES

Australia's youngest Federal politician was in the news again. **Andrew Jones**, of Adelaide, was fined 80 Pounds and disqualified from driving for four months. The arresting officer said that Mr Jones had made it known to him that he was a Federal MP, and implied that in the previous weeks he had been stopped by another officer, and had escaped penalty by talking to a Superintendent.

The officer ignored this information and proceeded with his duty of booking Jones.

Hollywood actress Jayne Mansfield was killed in a driving smash when her chauffeur-driven car went under a reticulated vehicle on the way to an engagement in New Orleans.

She had given an interesting interview days earlier. She announced her intention to study law at Oxford University, and said that it was her great ambition to become a solicitor in England. "I want to learn how to speak Oxford English. I adore England and the way they speak. I love the elegance of life there, and Englishmen, and the House of Commons. Everything sends me."

Two members of an English pop group, called **the Rolling Stones**, were gaoled on drug charges at Sussex in England. One was the group's leader, **Mick Jagger**, who was sent up for three months for possessing pep pills. The second was **Keith Richards** for allowing his house to be used for smoking Indian hemp.

HOLT'S PARTY

It was obvious to everyone here that President Johnson's party for Holt was a symbolic gesture of appreciation for Holt's full support of the Vietnam war. "All the way with LBJ" was supposedly a slogan that was supported by all Australia, and in dispute-plagued America, Johnson just had to reward such a loyal friend.

Of course, most commentary back home was cynical. The Letter below was typical.

Letters, Julie Meller. I am not surprised that Mr Holt described the Middle East crisis as a "lot of huffing and puffing." To those untutored to the rigours of a political life, it may seem a frivolous and inappropriate remark but after reading the "Herald's" account of the State banquet in honour of Mr and Mrs Holt, one realises the enormous program arranged for our Prime Minister and makes allowances for the occasional inept remark. This recent display of American hospitality at the

White House illustrates the progressive seduction of the Australian country cousin.

To the strains of "Tie Me Kangaroo Down," which seems somehow appropriate, Mr Holt again says "all the way with LBJ" and dutifully swallows some more of President Johnson's specially prepared ice-cream.

VIETNAM WAR AND CIVIL LIBERTIES

The executive of the RSL movement was conservative, and disciplinarian, and once it had made up its mind, it was loath to change it. It had decided that the sending of troops to Vietnam was in Australia's best interest, and was happy to express that view publicly. This was despite the fact that many of the rank and file members of the RSL were bitterly opposed to the fighting.

When a couple of members publicly said that they opposed the war, the NSW executive censured them and debated whether they should be expelled. The President went so far as to say that they were being subversive, amid other uncomplimentary words.

This drew the following responses.

Letters, Mary Ancich. All Australia must have been sickened by the action of the NSW State Council of the RSL in "disciplining" M Waddington and Ashley Pascoe for opposing its official policy on conscription and Vietnam conduct, apparently both subversive and ungentlemanly.

I would agree with Sir William Yeo that opposition is subversive, but, only for a totalitarian regime. In our society, frank and open dissension and discussion is a bulwark of democracy.

Letters, NX90199. At the last Federal election over 40 per cent of the votes were cast for the Australian

Labor Party's anti-conscription (for overseas service), anti-Vietnam involvement policy. As the membership of the RSL is a cross-section of the general public, it means that over 40 per cent of the membership would be opposed to our presence in Vietnam.

When I joined the RSL 23 years ago, I was led to believe that it was a non-political, non-sectarian organisation, a free forum for discussion. The Vietnam war is the most controversial issue today, not only in Australia, but in the United States as well, and if it cannot be discussed freely, without fear of expulsion, by the members who have fought for that very right, the RSL is no longer a free organisation.

Comment. Yeo was a strong leader who did many good things for the RSL. However, he did draw a lot of criticism during his long reign, and it was often said that his opinions were not as balanced or temperate as might have been expected from an important national figure.

ABORIGINES

The average white Australian had changed his attitude to Aborigines in the last 20 years. In the years around 1967, the Commonwealth set up an Office for Aboriginal Affairs, Aborigines and Torres Strait Islanders were now to be included in the Census, and soon the various States and the Commonwealth would be introducing measures designed to bring Aborigines towards equality.

But the flow of goodwill was patchy. Look for example at Bega below. This was a farming community, reasonably prosperous, and with only a relatively few natives, who seemed to be on the road to assimilation.

As an aside, I should mention that while there were many who argued that **assimilation** was a good thing, there was an equal number who said that it destroyed the heritage of the Aborigines, and left them without the tribal benefits that had served them well in the past.

Now, back to Bega.

Letters, Una Fitzhardinge. Some years go everyone living in Bega admired the vigour and enthusiasm which the community brought to the inauguration of the Bega-Littleton exchanges, one of the first such exchanges between an Australian town and one in the United States.

A fresh challenge has come to the Bega community: the Yes vote on Aboriginal rights at the recent referendum made the views of Australians on the subject quite clear; now the people of Bega are being asked, with other communities, to give a lead to the nation. The Aboriginal Welfare Board proposes to build modern houses for a number of Aboriginal families on blocks purchased from the Bega Glebe estate, which was subdivided and offered for sale some years ago by the Anglican parish authorities. The families already living on the Glebe estate, and the community as a whole, will thus be given the chance to show what charity, patience and understanding can do in assimilating these far from "new" citizens into the nation.

They welcomed and do welcome visitors from Littleton, Colorado; here is their chance to give a warm welcome to guests from nearer home. And once again the whole Australian nation will be watching their progress.

There was however, a different picture in outback Australia. In the sprawling country towns, the cattle spreads of the Northern Territory, in creeks and gullies around Alice Springs, in the deserts of our Centre, in fact in most areas of non-urbanised Australia, attitudes against Aborigines were a lot harder.

Politicians and white city voters could say and do what they liked, but there was a sizeable hard-core of whites, some with vested interests and some not, who still saw the Aborigines as an inferior race not to be mixed with.

Comment. So, when we sit back and glow satisfied, as we should, over the statutory improvements made in the later 1960's, we should remember that there remained quite a few people whose attitudes to Aborigines were still negative, and that the road to an equal footing would be long and hard. And that is how it remains today.

DOCTORS' FEES

Doctors were asking for an increase in the fees that they charge patients. It appears that since 1954, their fees had risen by over 100 per cent, while the average middle-class man had an increase of 30 per cent.

Against this, it should be remembered that doctors worked about 100 hours per week, compared to 40 to 50 for the average worker....

Then again, half the doctors' hours are on stand-by, and he may or may not be actually working in that period. **The debate gets more complicated, but it rages on, and you can see that a decision is no easy matter.**

JULY NEWS ITEMS

Trotting, or pacing as it is sometimes called, was very popular around Australia in 1967. **Night meetings under the stars were big attractions,** and the sums gambled were huge....

Drivers were free to whip their horses and they did so liberally at the close of races. But in NSW, racing authorities will **now ban drivers from using their own whips, and will issue standard whips**. These will be made of cane, and be four feet long and half an inch in diameter....

Previously private whips had been used, made of whalebone or fibreglass, and the length and diameter was at the discretion of the driver. It is said that the **new whips would be kinder to the horses**, and it is hoped and expected that other States will follow this lead.

The Post-Master General's Department will close some small Post Offices on Saturdays because they generate little revenue. Observers feared that this was **the thin edge of the wedge**, and that soon all Post Offices would be closed on Saturdays. **They were right...**

It also enhanced the new concept that user pays. That is, if a service cannot pay for itself, it should be dropped. The old idea of providing a public facility, paid for by taxes, and maybe running at a loss, was under challenge....

The user pays principle now dominates in some arenas, **particularly the banks.** Back in 1967, they thrived on the differences between the borrowing and lending rates. **Now they still get that, but also charge for every conceivable service as well.** We dopes are programmed to accept that.

Hollywood actress **Vivian Leigh** was found dead in her bed. She was famous for her role in *Gone with the Wind*, and for **her marriage to Laurence Olivier.** She had been suffering from TB and exhaustion. Sir Laurence at the moment has problems with prostate cancer....

It somehow interests me that she was **born in the fantasy world of Darjeeling**, the tea-growing centre in India.

Big things are happening in aviation. The normal return fare to England is $1,178. **Charter flight specialists are emerging** that charge $550 return for the same route....

They propose to use **Douglas DC8 jet airliners that seat 258 passengers**, and their big capacity and fast speed make this halving of the price possible. Travellers will need to be organised in groups to participate, and **will initially be relatives of persons who have previously migrated to Australia**.

The Australian Advisory Transport Board recommended that all new cars for 1969 have front-seat safety belts fitted. Rear-seat belts would be obligatory in all new cars from 1971....

Comment. Ridiculous twaddle. No Australian will ever consent to the fitting of such devices to his own car. There is such a thing as personal freedom.

NEW IMAGE WANTED

Letters, B May. While watching the TV broadcast of Australia Day at Expo 67, I was appalled to hear Bobby Limb continually referring to Australia as *Down Under*. While this expression may be commonly used overseas, to me it suggests the bottom of a hole or burial out of sight, and an image which should be destroyed and a new "On Top" image created.

To create this new "On Top" image, I would like to suggest to the people responsible for promoting Australia overseas that maps of the world, also globes of the world, be produced in reverse - that is the South Pole on top of the maps and globes. This, I feel, would create a tremendous amount of interest among our friends overseas.

Letters, Julie Melov. In the recent televised American interview, "Meet the Press," Mr Holt did not disappoint his critics. The Prime Minister warned against the dangers of Communist expansionism and strongly reaffirmed his support of President Johnson's policy in Vietnam.

Predictably, an interviewer was prompted to question Mr Holt about our enormous wheat sales to China. In reply our Prime Minister expressed a desire to establish points of contact between Australia and China by trade agreements and cultural exchanges.

That Mr Holt could reconcile these conflicting concepts cheerfully must have the American people wondering if their staunch ally really does walk on his head.

HERE'S A GOOD IDEA FOR BUILDING

Building restrictions that had crippled the house building industry for 25 years were being lifted in all States. This meant that families could build cottages, and that developers could start to create projects on a large scale.

This Letter was talking about the relatively low cost of building in brick, and inter alia he offered this opinion. **Letters, T Edwards, Secretary, Brick Manufacturers' Association.** Behind this apparently simple procedure, however, there is a tremendous amount of thought and research going on throughout the world. New building codes have been and are being evolved alongside new concepts in the technology of brickwork. One answer to Mr Bisset's question is **the apartment block, known here as "home units."** Such units are being built in Europe and the United States to a height of 17 or 18 stories. Cost-conscious engineers, architects and builders there, and more recently here in Australia, have proved beyond all doubt that "brick by brick" is by far the most economical form of construction of these giants of the housing field.

Comment. Of course, apartment blocks and flats were **already common** in our cities, but **home units were not**. The idea of having a number of people club together into body corporates and develop and then manage a number of units under a Strata Title was new to Australia. I hardly need to say that the concept has grown and grown so that the skylines of our cities are dominated by the giants that the writer referred to.

SOME THOUGHTS ON PAPUA NEW GUINEA

There is a lot of talk about how we should manage Papua New Guinea. We administered that nation under a mandate from the United Nations, which had set standards and time frames for us to develop the land. We were doing this quite well, but we were starting to ask what its future should be.

There were two main arguments. **The first** said that PNG should become a nation in its own right, independent of Australia. Advocates for this did recognise that this would take time and that, before and after separation, the new PNG would have to rely heavily on Australian support.

The second argument wanted PNG to become a Territory, or even a State of Australia, which meant that Canberra would have control of its affairs for a long time. Intuitively this had little appeal for New Guineans, but was much supported by vested interests in Australia.

The *SMH* weighed into this argument. It said that to accept that PNG should become a Territory was wrong. One good argument it raised was that "such a solution would satisfy only one generation of Papuans. It is incompatible with the **whole spirit of nationalism**, and there are already the first faint stirrings of nationalism in PNG. **Even if most Papuans today were prepared to accept absorption into Australia, the Papuans of tomorrow would see it as a betrayal.**"

A writer to the *SMH* did not accept this view. He said that Australia **could** make provision for PNG to secede if in future it wanted to. He also said that "independence and nationalism are popular words, but if they are followed to their end in the South Pacific, we shall have separate nations of Papua New Guinea, the Solomons, Fiji, the New Hebrides, New Caledonia, and so on."

As an aside, I might mention that he was correct in that. That indeed **has** happened, but it does not seem to be the bogey he feared.

At this time, the *SMH* rejoiced a little. It was able to report that the Government and Minister had at last made a decision. But here are its words, and you can see what it thought about the attempts so far to find solutions.

Editorial. Because the Australian Government refused to reveal its attitude towards bringing Papua-New Guinea to independence as a State, sections of opinion within the Territory have been encouraged to look to this as their goal. This has confused the direction of political movement and diverted political energies into useless bypaths. The Government, ill served by its Territories Ministers, carries a heavy responsibility for what must appear as a deliberate misleading of the Papuans but what was probably no more than its customary inability to make up its mind about anything to do with New Guinea's future.

Now, at long last, in the first reasonably clear statement of a Ministerial career remarkable for its obscurantism, Mr Barnes has ruled the Seventh State solution out of court. Although in his own inimitable style, Mr Barnes still managed to spray about a little confusion and uncertainty, his audience was left in no real doubt that **the present Government at any rate would not countenance Australian Statehood for Papua-New Guinea**.

Leaving aside **the delightful snide references**, it appears that the authorities had at last made up their minds. PNG would not become a State, but would rather be led to **independence**. And this is what happened. That nation, while still heavily dependent on Australia in some matters, now has its voice in its own right and, while at times it niggles Australia, this has been achieved with **a measure of harmony that few other parts of the world have seen**.

PNG DOGS

Before I leave PNG, I would like to give you a Letter that illustrates that how big the gulf was that separated PNG and Australia. Technically, PNG was under our protection, and the Torres Strait was only a few miles wide. But, in terms of administration, we could have been on different planets.

Letters, A Jones. Under provisions of the Quarantine Act, 1908-61, dogs and cats may be imported into Australia only from the United Kingdom, Northern Ireland, Republic of Ireland or New Zealand.

An Australian temporarily residing in New Guinea could not return to Australia with his pet dog. He must first consign his pet to England to enter quarantine for six months. Afterwards it must be shipped to Australia to undergo a further quarantine period of 120 days.

Such a prolonged period involves the owner in a very great expense, apart from the fact that nearly a year passes before he can repossess his pet.

It is suggested that a modification of these regulations should be made.

Territory pet dogs and cats should be allowed to accompany their owners to the mainland and spend a suitable quarantine period in Australia instead of having first to travel to England.

The opinion of the veterinary panel of State and Commonwealth veterinarians is that the direct importation of pets from Papua-New Guinea is safe, subject to the introduction of normal quarantine procedures.

The problem of abandoned pets would largely be overcome if Territory residents returning to live in Australia could take their pets with them.

THE YEAR OF THE POST CODE

Officially, post codes on envelopes have been tested and are now required on every piece of mail posted. The new Mail Sorting Facility is in operation at Redfern in Sydney, and will electronically handle much of Sydney's mail. But other parts of Australia must also fall into line, and after a period of tolerance, all items without a code will be returned to sender (if they show a return address with a post code) or to the Dead Letter Office.

Postal workers for years have dreaded the introduction of this piece of automation, knowing that it would reduce employment in this field. They spent a fair percentage of their working hours striking and refusing to work as the threat grew. Now, they have seen that introduction of this piece of automation world-wide is inevitable, and have accepted the PMG's offer to roll with the punches.

To celebrate Post Code Day, I give you four Letters addressing the subject.

Letters, N Arlen. Now that the Australian Post Office has devised a way to facilitate its service by introducing a postcode for every place in Australia, surely its method could be further simplified by cutting out entirely the need to write the name of the district concerned, e.g.: to Mr John Brown, 27 Outlook Drive, 2108 NSW.

Letters, A Chester. It surprises me that there have not been more protests concerning this latest bureaucratic brain child. The amount of time which will be consumed in referring to the booklet and typing or writing a number on every envelope used every day in the whole of Australia will be colossal.

The whole purpose seems to be to suit the convenience of the electronic marvels installed at the Redfern Mail Exchange and other places which do not seem to have been a resounding success to date.

Letters, Miriam Patton. Having worked for an hour with the new postcode booklet, I have come to the conclusion that the Postal Department wishes to subsidise both the optical industry and the manufacturers of tranquilising drugs.

Has the Department considered the thousands of office workers who will have to transfer millions of postcode numbers to ledger cards, mailing lists, etc, apart from those people whose eyesight is not perfect?

Letters, Fred Burke. In my opinion the postcode is advanced solely for the purpose of buttressing the dubious efficiency of the electronic sorting monster recently installed in the Redfern Mail Exchange.

I fail to see that the addition of a postcode will conduce in the slightest to the more speedy delivery of a letter, particularly if it is addressed to a private box number and the name of the city, town or State is clearly shown on the envelope.

HOSPITAL TYRANTS

Letters, John Gilmour. Egyptian mummies have nothing on me and other fellow hospital bed-making victims. Why in the name of all that's holy must every nurse, every matron, every hospital insist that the blankets on the beds of their victims should be tucked a foot at the bottom and almost 18 inches up each side so that the suffering patient suffers even more by weight, constriction and worst of all cold on neck and shoulders - and, for that matter, both sides - down the air channel each side?

The Letter above brought back memories of 1967. My sister was by then a nursing sister in a hospital, well on her way to becoming a matron. She had done her four years apprenticeship as a nurse and was now taking special courses to improve her nursing skills.

She would regale us with stories of the matrons she came into contact with, and her stories brought out different stories from others who had contact with hospital hierarchies.

The control that matrons had of their hospitals was nothing short of military. Yes, the nurses had to tuck those sheets in, **precisely**, so that the patient could not move, and if they didn't make the bed properly, then there was some cross to bear. On top of that, **the patients and families were bullied beyond belief.** If a husband and wife wanted the husband to attend the birth of their child, the answer was emphatically no. If a sick and frightened child wanted to see his mum, then visiting time was one hour per day, no exceptions.

Nurses lived in quarters for much of their traineeship. They were on a nine-o'clock curfew, no phone calls after eight, no visitors, and no standing up for basic rights.

Hospitals, to coin a military phrase, were tight ships. **There was some need for this.** Trainee nurses living away from home needed to be controlled, some patients if left undisciplined would take the earth, some drunken dads must be kept out of birthing rooms.

Comment. But to me, these were the exceptions. They could have been treated as such, to the benefit of all. Later matrons have shown that this can be done,

Second comment, added a few days after writing all the above. I am surprised how much animosity I have towards old-style matrons. I think it is just part of the lingering resentment that a youth feels when his much-loved sister and family is bullied. **I am not even certain that I am being fair to these matrons.** Still, I won't cut the comments, and I think they will ring bells with many of you. **Anyway, you decide.**

SHOPPING HOURS

If you are a shopper, it is nice to be able to shop most hours of the day. If you work in a shop, then you are most happy to work from nine to five and have Saturday off. Except that you will work on Sundays if you get double time. If you are a motorist, then you want to be able to buy petrol early in the morning and late at night. But that is no good if you **work** in a service station. And so on. And on.

Everyone had their own ideas of what shopping hours should be, but most people were agreed that they should be liberalised to provide greater access for shoppers. So, now pressure was growing for longer hours for shoppers, and different wage scales for workers. Arguments came and went, and resolutions seemed hopeless.

Unions were in the forefront of the no-change movement because of the fatigue that changes would bring to workers. **Though**, if paid overtime was conceded, that fatigue would surely vanish. Petrol stations were frightened of being robbed if they opened till midnight, but not at long weekends because the robbers would be on holidays then.

This was a galling issue for all concerned. The corner store came into it. At the moment, there were few supermarkets as we now know them, just a collection of a few shops in a mall. Many corner stores were still literally mum-and-dad stores, with only a few casuals for peak hours. They were all caught up in this long-running battle to find a balance between the varying positions.

The Letter below simply illustrates **the mess** that this arena was in. I advise you **not to worry about the detail**, just read it to see what I mean about **the mess**.

Letters, R Nicholls, Traders' Association of NSW.

Objections have been raised over changes to retail laws. Objections stem from the law amendments of 1965, which were aimed principally at freeing small shops from controls preventing them from meeting the public's needs at weekends and homecoming times.

The State Government did this through a new small-shop classification, but decreed that small traders would be ineligible unless they ceased to stock green groceries, bar two varieties. Most of them can't do this because it alienates their customers and inhibits the convenient service which is the very basis of their business existence. It also diverts to greengrocers a share of trade which they could not otherwise have expected. No wonder their Association opposes any change to that satisfactory arrangement.

Thus all but a minority of traditional "corner stores" are still involved in the cloak-and-dagger conditions which the amendments sought to abolish.

Greengrocers argue that stores classified as small shops are allowed to trade after their own 7.30pm closing time, ignoring the fact that most of them close before that time because the homecoming trade is over.

Nor do they mention that, prior to the new classification, greengrocers had for years been lawfully able to trade for at least 30 hours weekly longer than these corner stores - selling in that time a range of their groceries and ancillary lines. A masterful demonstration of having your cake and eating it too.

Country greengrocers may lawfully trade until 11.30pm. What rubbish to talk of unfair competition when only half an hour of the day is left to compete unfairly. Yet small traders in diverse places like Dubbo, Leeton, and Cowra are still having as much trouble with inspections as they did under the old "Stone Age" laws.

Comment. The corner store, as we know, gradually gave way to local malls and then later the giant shopping centres. These changes all brought their problems. For example, what wages and hours should a junior in McDonalds get? Can older women become check-out chicks? Should motorists pour their own petrol, or have driveway attendants do it for them? These questions came and went.

When you look back at it, the changes that have occurred in all aspects of retailing in the last 50 years are enormous. **This is social change at the grass roots**, and for anyone seeking to change the world today, it would be wise to take a long-term view.

WHAT ABOUT A BIG BANG?

An Australian oil exploration company, **Magellan Oil**, will seek permission to **explode a nuclear device in Central Australia** in the Amadeus Basin. They plan an underground explosion that will create a mound of rubble, but no contamination or radiation will reach the surface.

They will need **all sorts of approvals** both here and in America to do this.

In fact, these approvals were never given, and **the idea lapsed for a while**. A few years later there were voices that wanted to **drop a bomb on the coast of our North West Cape to create a Harbour** that **tides** would flow in and out of. This movement would be used to generate electricity. **Again, the idea lapsed.**

NEWS AND VIEWS

Letters, Laurie Douglas. It is no wonder that there is discontent and low morale among some sections of Public Servants when one is confronted with the "stunt" that happened to the majority of staff at North Ryde Psychiatric Centre last payday, and no doubt to other Public servants also.

On an average, staff were short 45 cents in their pay packets compared with the previous fortnight's pay, and on querying this we were told that we are now in "a leap year financial year and our salary is based on an annual rate which in turn is based on a 365-day year." If this practice continues it means that every four years we are paid less fortnightly than the previous three years. How bad can the NSW Public Service Board get?

Letters, Helen McCauliff. Is there any law that says that as soon as a family gets their third child, it must get a station wagon?

AUGUST NEWS ITEMS

Rolling Stones' **Mick Jagger** and Keith Richards had their **gaol sentences quashed by the Appeals Court.** While it found them guilty, it gave them release **on condition they were good boys for three months.** Jagger promised he would be. Lots of teenage girls **squealed** from the public gallery when he was released. **The girls' mothers moaned**, no doubt.

Arthur Stace was a name that few of us have heard of. But any old-timer in Sydney will remember his **artwork This consisted of the word** *Eternity* **written in chalk in perfect copper-plate on the pavements of Sydney's streets.** Always writing in the middle of the night, he wrote his one word composition in a big range of Sydney's suburbs **for 34 years....**

He started when a Baptist preacher converted him to Christianity. The preacher said that he wished he could shout *Eternity* through the streets of Sydney. **Stace did the next best thing and wrote** *Eternity* **everywhere.** He died recently.

There is a young bloke pressing for much-needed reform of the Labor Party. The Party has not held office for 17 years, and looks to have no chance of getting back into power unless it comes to grips with the post-socialist world. But the old guard, led by Arthur Calwell, keeps backing losers....

I can't promise you anything but this young bloke, **Gough Whitlam,** seems to have a head of steam, and is winning Labor Party supporters in unexpected quarters.

Though, he has a huge task ahead if he is to move the Labor Party. **He will probably be just a flash in the pan. Still, keep an eye on him for the moment at least.**

Riots by negroes in the American south and along the east coast, up to New York, had been going on for a month. **The death toll was over 200, and increasing every night.** **A new development** is happening in New York with gangs of **organised white vigilantes** going out at night determined to exact revenge for the recent violence. This **is increasing, rather than stopping, the violence**, and it shows every sign of spreading nation-wide.

Vancouver, in Canada's British Columbia, has **lured Australian   teachers** there by placing enticing ads that offer better pay and conditions. **A boatload of 200 teachers**, and their families, arrived this week. This exodus is seen as a threat to Australia's education system.

A reminder that the **battles in Vietnam are still going on. Six Australian soldiers were killed** at the weekend, and 15 injured in a Vietcong raid. No further details were made available.

The War! What war? Twenty-two years after WWII, **Japan is now taking more of our exports** than any other country. They buy iron ore, coal and sugar. Generally, **Britain was our second best customer,** while **the USA was a distant third.** In any case, **the threat presented by Britain joining the Common Market was not as big** as when they first started talking about it.

A Mrs Jones in Victoria **gave birth successfully to quads**. The Government agreed to give her **a sum of $10 a week to supplement Child Endowment payments**. This would allow her to meet costs of feeding and clothing the ankle biters.

The Beatles' effect. A 14-year-old boy in Victoria **had grown his hair to Beatle length**. The Headmaster of his school ordered him to get it cut. He did so, but his **father alleged in the Supreme Court that the boy had lost confidence and began to stutter as a consequence**. The father is asking the Court to declare that the boy's rights were infringed under the Education Act. The hearing was adjourned.

The Bee Gees were doing well in England. But **the work-permits** of the two Australian-born members of the Group **will expire soon** and they will be sent out. The other three members, carrying Australian passports, were born in Britain, so they could stay if they wanted.... But **all five will stay together as a Group**, and will next settle in America.

A new Australian stamp showing two naked women will go on sale in a few days. It is to celebrate the World Conference on Gynecology to be held in Sydney.

A long-haired 6-year-old boy in Indonesia, suckled and raised by apes in Central Java, has been brought back to civilisation to learn how to talk and walk like a human. At the moment **he does not talk, appears dumb, and walks on all fours**. He refused to eat rice, but ate greens....

Troops captured the **"ape-boy"** by scaring off the ape pack with shots over their heads, and snatching the boy when one ape tried to carry him off.

The State Executive of the NSW RSL reversed its decision on the two Members who **had been suspended for speaking out on Vietnam.** They claim that they did so on legal advice. They would have been truer and wiser to say that they backed down because of **public pressure in favour of the two men expelled.**

In London, **86-year-old Lord Stanhope**, 13th Earl of Chesterfield and a Knight of the Garter, lamented that, while the Queen has lots of properties, **the children have nothing.** So, on his death, in his will he made **a small provision for Prince Charles....**

He left for Charles his 17th Century home, Chevening Manor in Kent, and its 3,500 acre estate. The manor has 50 rooms, and a 4-acre lake in the grounds, and good hunting facilities....

It all sounds nice, but pity the other children of Elizabeth. **Nothing at all, so far. Poor buggers.**

NSW is having a troublesome **outbreak of hepatitis.** This is a disease, new to the public, who **find it strange** to **wash hands if they are not dirty.**

A survey of roadside litter found that, on the hundred miles of highway between Sydney and Newcastle, there was an **average of one piece of litter every twenty yards.** It also found that on that same stretch of highway, there were **two litter bins, both over-full.**

AIRPORT TAX

Here is a good suggestion. Surely no one would object to its implementation. Only $1 per flight.

Letters, D Steley. With all the talk of different taxes, may I suggest an airport tax? I would levy interstate and intrastate passengers departing from an airport $1; international passengers would be levied $2.

Terminals, runways and facilities at airports are an enormous expense to the Government and should be paid for by the people using those facilities.

Comment. It is nice to see that this tax has been so popular with passengers that it has grown to $55 per flight. This might have something to do with the provision of parking facilities and the availability of food and drink at

But hang on a minute. Passengers have to pay for these too. And they seem to cost a fortune.

Maybe then it is just another case of **user pays**. Through the nose, I might suggest.

NEW LAWS FOR HOMOSEXUALS

In 1957, Britain's Lord Wolfenden handed down a report from his Committee that studied homosexuality in that nation. In a very controversial judgement, he recommended that most laws that restricted men (only) from having sexual exchanges with consenting adults be removed from the statute books. This matter was argued steadily for a decade, until July 1967, when his suggestions were passed into law.

In Australia, we as a nation were a long way from following suit. Most people here were opposed to accepting homosexuality. Perhaps they quoted the Bible, or their parents. Perhaps they just said it was unnatural, or perhaps they thought it was unsafe or dangerous to children. There were dozens of reasons. Then there was constant ridicule, with so-called comics getting certain laughs with references to limp wrists, and with parodies of camp posture and gait. There were gangs of youths who spent weekend nights poofter bashing, and police who spent their nights in public lavatories hoping to catch an offender. All of this activity, and much more, went on in Australia with scarcely any objection.

The legislation in Britain (but not Scotland) started people here thinking and talking. And there were some signs emerging of more accepting attitudes. A couple of Protestant churches said we should look at the whole situation, with the intention of reform. Then the *SMH* weighed in with a strong Editorial.

The Editor pointed out that France, and most of Christian Europe, had removed restraints on homosexuality long ago by the Code Napoleon. He said that the recent British changes had the approval of the Archbishop of Canterbury and most churches, and a big majority of Parliamentarians. He recognised that it would take much courage for our own legislators to act on this matter. He concluded "we must ask whether any law at all has the right to tell free men how they should give expression in private to their most intimate longings and needs."

This view had was accepted by some with caution.

Letters, Gordon Cooper. It was pleasing to read the sub-leader on the law and homosexuals. Reform of the law, to remove from its ambit sexual relations between consenting male adults, is certainly long overdue in NSW. I rather suspect, however, that while some senior members of the NSW Parliament have indicated that they favour a liberalisation of the law applying to homosexuals, most members of the Legislature would not have the courage or the foresight to support such a reform.

But there was plenty of outspoken opposition.

Letters (Rev) H Brown. Your leader of last Friday is characteristic of so much of the present day's unhealthy and abominable thinking that I trust you will be fair-minded enough to allow me, on behalf of many others, to make as strong a protest as possible.

Such a moral landslide has taken place that Church leaders, parliamentarians, newspaper editors, etc., can almost flippantly describe as "disease," "weakness," etc., what God in no mistaken terms calls SIN. In His word, God speaks of homosexuality in the following terms: "Thou shalt not lie with mankind as with womankind: it is an abomination." (Leviticus 18:22.) This was the sin that was very largely responsible for the overthrow of Sodom and Gomorrah. The Apostle Paul could have been writing in 1967 when he wrote to the Romans, "Similarly, the men, turning from natural intercourse with women, were swept into lustful passions with one another. Men with men performed these shameful horrors, receiving, of course, in their own personalities the consequences of sexual perversity. And even as they did not like to retain God in their knowledge, God gave them over to a reprobate mind."

Your allusion to the Archbishop of Canterbury supporting the Bill in the House of Lords, and to the Presbyterian Assembly of NSW and the Methodist General Conference condoning these things, is not the slightest bit impressive, but only serves to emphasise the apostate age in which we are living.

Even though, as suggested in your article, "the police will not have to search the public lavatories any more," there will be no mitigation at the judgment bar of God, for "All things are naked and opened unto the eyes of Him with Whom we have to do."

Reverend Brown's Letter unfortunately set the tone of the responses for the next few weeks. He had fallen back on quotes from the Bible to make his argument, and he initially got Biblical Letters in response. Some people quoted different parts of the Bible to support or mainly discredit his views, others talked about the Christian ideals of tolerance and basically minding your own business, and others talked about hell and damnation for transgressors.

But there were quite a few sensible responses to the Letters over a month or so. By this I mean that some writers talked about the essence of homosexuality. What caused it, could it be cured, were mothers at fault for cloying too much, could drugs fix it, were psychologists any use, would counselling help, would prison effect a cure, should we pity the practitioners, could we just ignore it and leave people make their own choice? Some of these questions might seem almost silly in these our later years, but at the time they were novel and showed that people here were thinking more than ever before about the matter.

The issue, though, continued to quietly fester for a long time before any legislative action was taken. The States started to pass more liberal laws in **the early eighties** and by the end of the decade, everyone was a lot freer to do their own thing than they had been before. **Then**, we British types can say with pride, we had caught up with the licentious French after a trifling 180 years.

RIOTS IN THE US

The rioting in the US was widespread and had been going on for months. The National Guard had been called out many times in many States, hundreds had been killed and maimed, and rioting and looting were happening daily somewhere in the nation. The white authorities were scratching their heads hard about what caused it, and what to do about it, and were acting piecemeal to control it.

Australians were watching this with interest, especially given the recent bally-hoo about peace-loving prosperous America saving the world from the low-life Reds.

Note that this was also a time when there was a lot of agitation for us to relax, or remove, our White Australia Policy.

Letters, K Faulkes. Mr Brownlee's argument in support of the White Australia Policy rests on the facile assumptions that race and colour in themselves were the causes of the US riots, and that the American situation can be applied to Australia. Both assumptions are false.

The American agony is part of the legacy of the introduction of the Negro as slave labour, of the savagery and bitterness of the Civil War, and more immediately of the resulting generations of denial to the Negro of economic and social justice, and of his intolerable living conditions. No such factors need bar the integration of Asian or other races into the Australian community, should we discard the White Australia policy.

It is inevitable that the policy must go. World opinion, the articulate conscience of thinking Australians, and the exigencies of living and trading with our Asian neighbours demand it. But the introduction into Australia of other races need not mean the beginning of racial friction. This is shown by the example of multi-racial societies such as Hawaii and Brazil, and indeed by our own experience with the thousands of Asian students now in Australia.

Surveys in England have shown that initial racial prejudice is broken down by actual contact with persons of other races. We have the opportunity now to begin the introduction of suitable Asian immigrants on a graduated and carefully considered basis, to ensure that problems which have arisen in other countries due to   planning errors (concentration of coloured immigrants in low-status occupations, inadequate housing, etc.) do not occur here.

Let us suppose that initially under such a program 5 per cent of our total number of immigrants each year were to be Asian. Does anyone seriously believe that Australians are so blindly bigoted and intolerant that racial disturbances would inevitably result?

Other writers chipped in. They reminded us that the large scale immigration of races had sometimes been successful. The Japanese in Hawaii was quoted as such. One writer said we needed population, and that migration of Asians might give us a slightly brown look that would not be so offensive to the Asian hordes. Another suggested that if we put a rising sun on one corner of our flag, the Japanese at least would see us as willing to accommodate their culture. This brought a response that our White policy was matched by their brown and yellow policies, and that Asians' restrictions on whites were more severe than our restrictions on coloureds.

It was good healthy dialogue at a time when our walls against Asian immigrants were falling, and when our grossest injustices to Aborigines were being reduced.

One writer summed it up when he said that, in reference to the coloured riots in America, and the world, we **somehow** "had got out of gaol", and that our continued harmony was more by good luck than good management. He added that we should consciously follow humanitarian policies, in a world-wide context, lest we are not so lucky in the future.

NEWS AND VIEWS

Letters, Estelle Rickards. Why, when flowers are presented to actresses, dancers or singers at the end of a performance in this city, are they almost invariably bundles of gladioli, in or out of season, encased in cellophane? It does seem sad when flowers, especially at this time of the year, are in good supply and not quite so expensive as at some other times and in some other places, more use cannot be made of the variety we have.

It can't be beyond the skill of our florists to devise attractive and secure arrangements of even daisies or dandelions, done with imagination which would not have to be wrapped up in light-catching and colour-distorting shiny paper like vegetables in a supermarket.

When the danseuses from the Paris Opera Ballet after the first performance here were each presented with an almost identical wrapped bunch of the inevitable "glads," it was quite impossible for the bouquets to be held gracefully while bows were taken. They had to be hurriedly placed on a platform at the back of the stage and the pretty gesture of plucking a single flower to give to the male dancers wasn't possible either; even if a bloom could be detached from its fellows a single gladiolus does little for the male lapel.

Letters, W Smith, Blackheath. An injured hikers' companion gave the injured hiker copious drinks of water although he was suffering and showing all the signs of continuing internal haemorrhage. He was dead when we reached him.

And this week-end I saw where a slip of a girl had tried to ford a swollen creek with five feet of water in it in Megalong Valley, when she and her companions could have walked to Blackheath via Hargreaves Lookout by another fire trail. Result loss of one young life. On Tuesday I saw where another girl had tried to swim the Cox's River when it was one hundred and fifty feet wide, fifteen feet deep and travelling at least 30 knots, taking with it complete river oaks weighing probably five tons. There was no need for this girl to swim this river. Help was on the way from both sides of the river. If they couldn't be taken out over the river, they would have been taken out overhead on the Black Range fire trail.

These hikers or walkers do not know the areas they are walking in and therefore don't know alternative routes. Most of them appear to be untrained in basic First Aid. I've no doubt denials of this will come from all sorts of organisations. But the fact remains that in the last five years we have had to rescue Queen's Scouts, Rover Scouts, bushwalkers from most big clubs and numerous independent walkers. And I think the time has arrived for something to be done as J Heesh suggested in Saturday's "Herald."

SEPTEMBER NEWS ITEMS

The Federal Government has moved **to ban the import of the drugs that can be used to make LSD**. Little did they realise that many years later, about a dozen people would be arrested each week for illegally importing drugs, and that **back-yard laboratories** would make them into pills and the like....

Nor did they dream that **the ordering of the drugs from overseas would take just one minute on the internet. The whole industry has sped up**, and **that efficiency surely benefits us all.**

A woman parking inspector in Darwin, an ex-police officer, **has been fining doctors** for illegally parking when not actually visiting patients. She has also been **fining doctors' wives for using Red Cross stickers** on their cars when doing household shopping....

She has recently been **waking inhabitants of caravans at 4.30am** if they are illegally parked overnight at beaches. Although they all voluntarily move off each day at day-break, **she claims to be just doing her job. This is big news in Darwin**, the local newspapers are critical of her, and the Council says it will investigate.

In Australia, at the moment, if **a major court-based legal decision is disputed**, it may be that **our High Court will allow an appeal, and that must go to the British Privy Council**. In the past 20 years, there have been 28 such appeals made....

The Federal Government has now announced it will **reduce the number of appeals by about half**. This will later make way for **all** such decisions to be made by our High Court, and **cut our links to another British institution**.

Local Councils round the nation had been given grants by the States and Commonwealth to provide free library services to their locals. Up till now, the librarians had been free to choose books without interference. They adopted the policy of **not providing books that were currently on the Commonwealth Censorship Board's banned list....**

Ashfield Council in Sydney has decreed that **if a book had ever been banned**, they would not stock it. The Council adopted a further policy that it would **ban any book that it found offensive**. They voted for this to "save our youth from corruption...."

Many people were up in arms. They thought that these 1967 Councillors did not have the education or experience to become censors. **"What do these Councillors know that the Censorship Board does not know?"** "Bernie Toner is a Councillor. He can't read or write."

The American yacht *Intrepid* beat the Australian challenger in the America's Cup. The score was four to zero. The name of the Australian vessel was *Dame Pattie*. Can you remember why **that** name was chosen?

200,000 kangaroos were shot by professional hunters in NSW last year. Their skins and carcases are sold to meatworks and to furriers. From now, the first 10 cents of any such sale will go as a levy to the NSW taxation authorities.

PARAPLEGICS

The treatment of **paraplegics** in the nation was patchy. The Letter below talks about the good work being done in North Sydney, while there were also Letters that told a different story in other parts of the nation.

In any case, the accommodation for these patients was **everywhere** recognised as being as bad as that described below.

Letters, R Moores. While the Royal North Shore Hospital Paraplegic Unit has a wonderful reputation for the treatment and rehabilitation of paraplegics and quadriplegics, the buildings where this is carried out are a disgrace to a modern hospital.

The unit consists of four adjoining cottages, three for use as wards and one for physiotherapy and occupational therapy. This latter cottage, about the size of a one-bedroom house, is so overcrowded that patients have to be treated outside when it is fine, and if it rains they can only receive partial treatment due to inadequate room.

The three wards house 17 patients in various stages of rehabilitation. These wards are dark, dingy little cubby-holes, like ovens in summer and ice-boxes in winter. Even spinal units in famine-struck India and war-torn Congo have better facilities.

It has now been decided that a new unit will be built, when somewhere can be found to put it. Some people favour the idea of an autonomous unit, attached to the hospital but away from it, and others say it should be part of stage two of the new hospital, to be started sometime in the future. Whichever course is decided upon, it will be years before anything is started.

It is recognised by all leading authorities on paraplegia and quadriplegia that you do not **only** need to heal the broken bones of the patients, but also you must rehabilitate them as well. This means that they must be able to cope with the world around them when they leave hospital. They must be able to look after themselves, communicate with other people and able to work.

This ability to lead a reasonably normal existence must be relearned by the patients, and the staff are the people who must teach them.

In the present depressing atmosphere of the existing quarters even the most dedicated members of the staff find it difficult to do their job properly, and the patients often wonder what they ever did to society to end up in this little replica of nineteenth-century bureaucracy called a modern hospital.

Letters, Elizabeth Cooper. In this so-called affluent society, it is beyond comprehension that these disabled people should be housed in such unsuitable conditions.

Recently I went to see my son, who, I found, had been sent to the paraplegic unit from the very busy and overcrowded men's surgical ward to await discharge in a few days. I was appalled at the conditions I found him in.

Surely these people, whose morale, by the very nature of their illness, must at times be very low, would be helped if they were in more cheerful surroundings instead of being in what would appear to be the oldest, darkest, dingiest and most poorly kept buildings in the hospital grounds.

Personal Comment. I can tell you that the bad conditions were **not** caused because the local authorities and hospital staff were stupid, useless, or uncaring. It was caused by a shortage of money and resources. This is not the place to bemoan that this huge nation was pushed to its limit to create and mend its infrastructure, and that if money went to one purpose, it could not go to another. It happened, sadly, that paraplegics' accommodation was at the end of the pecking order. It is one of our realities of life that one way to improve its position was to write more and more agitating Letters like the ones above.

CENSOR IN THE LIBRARY

There were many writers who protested about the Ashfield Council Library's decision to add itself to the list of censors. Most of the resulting Letters were more or less straight forward, such as the one below which, as you might recognise, is a bit sarcastic.

Letters, H Inglis. The Ashfield Council is quite right to censor its library books. We have State and Federal censorship (which is now unluckily in process of co-ordination) so why not municipal censorship? In this business of protecting people's morals there is efficiency in numbers.

If we had to struggle along with only one censor, we should never know how good or badly he was doing his job because there would be nothing with which to compare his work and its results. If Ashfield purifies its library, then we shall be able to compare the morals of the residents of that delectable suburb with the morals of those who reside in uncensored or differently censored areas, and so decide what quantity and quality of censorship produces the right kind of morals!

When enough councils follow Ashfield and enough case studies are assembled, processed and graphed, then a pattern of censor-induced moral conduct will surely emerge so that we may, at last, **call censorship a true science**, and so give the lie to those cavillers who say that it is just so much hopeful magic which serves only to make the magician-censors feel good and everybody else anxiously to look for books they would otherwise hardly bother about.

But there were a few others, obviously with a good knowledge of literature. These were deeply offended by the Council's move, and wrote long Letters to express their distress. I enclose one such below, again sarcastic, but I warn you that some people may find the content offensive, so skip it if you like. I would not like to corrupt our oldies in any way.

Letters, P Farrell. After the publicity given to Alderman Crawford over his recent, and praiseworthy, censoring of certain books, I feel it should be brought to the public notice that there are others, of whom I am one, also bent on keeping from the public any books, which they might find obscene or shocking in any way. On this point I feel that the Censorship Board has not been doing its job properly - I have been investigating some books myself.

Mr William Shakespeare's works are on sale everywhere, any child may read them - in fact they are encouraged to - yet this man's works should be banned! They are the work of a twisted mind - a fact which should be obvious to all right-thinking Australians. For those who persist in thinking that Mr Shakespeare ever wrote anything of merit, literature which is the product of a perverted mind cannot be meritorious and Mr Shakespeare's mind is clearly perverted.

"His hand, that yet remains upon her breast" is a disgusting line and obviously pornographic.

Even the title of the work from which it was taken, "The Rape of Lucrecea," suggests this. Further, in "Julius Caesar," in which he writes about anarchy and the fall of a dictator, Calpurnia says in a speech: "Giving myself a voluntary wound here in the thigh." This not only has strong sexual overtones (implied by the word "thigh") but the "voluntary wound" is evidence of masochistic tendencies.

Sexuality and masochism are obscene, but Mr Shakespeare's perversions continued unabated - in "Twelfth Night" one of the main characters, Viola, is a transvestite. And "Two Gentlemen of Verona"... Well, the title itself condemns this play. Thus in only a few of this man's works we have homosexuality, transvestism, masochism and pornography. One wonders what kind of a person Mr Shakespeare is.

In the light of all this evidence, the Commonwealth Censorship Board still does not see its way to banning all this man's works. To my knowledge they have never been on the banned lists - they are not even marked as pornographic in our public libraries. Without these slim protections even the people of Ashfield are being subjected to this man's insidious influence. Mr Shakespeare and all his perverted works must be destroyed; the public must be made to realise this. For my part, if ever Mr Shakespeare attempts to set foot on our shores, I shall do everything in my power to prevent it.

FROG-GATE

This little Letter below stirred up a flood of responses.

Letters, Colin Simpson. I wish to protest against the frog-jumping contest now being held at a leading Sydney store. Hundreds of small boys are being encouraged to bring in frogs. What will happen to the hundreds of hapless frogs, wrenched from their natural watery habitats and carried foodless into the city in cardboard and plastic containers, can be imagined, as can all the prodding to test their prowess as jumpers.

This is cruelty, and no amount of "they're only frogs" and "it's all in fun" rationalisation can make this merchandising stunt less than cruelty.

I have had a charge account at this department store for 30-odd years. I am closing this account, and do not propose to buy anything there any more - unless the sensibilities of the management take a jump in the right direction and this frog thing is called off.

Comment. Before I move to the responses, I must say that on reading this I was reminded that many years ago in England I was in a nice country pub, and it was holding its **weekly dwarf tossing event**. Dwarfs, in certain weight and height categories, made themselves available, and were whirled and then thrown several yards across the saloon. The dwarf who went the furthest won the prize for himself and the thrower. I mention too that this was in no way sexist, and there were very competent female throwers and some very delicate lady dwarfs who made excellent projectiles.

There was some local objection to this as lowering the image of dwarfs, but the vast majority of them enjoyed it thoroughly because it involved them in **the general community that normally excluded them**. Also, they got paid by the pub, and their medical bills were paid by their National Health Insurance Scheme.

This sport persisted quietly in England for dozens of years. Then the Americans picked it up and made it into public spectacles. This got it too far away from the local pub scene and, before long, pubic opinion was ablaze, and it was banned in most places in the US. As far as I know, the fine body of throwers and projectiles suffered a consequent similar fate in England, and it appears to have disappeared.

Though I did notice, about the turn of the Century, that a pub in Brisbane was drawing Thursday-night crowds with such events.

In any case, turning back to frogs, many writers came to their aid.

Letters, Alma Kingsmill. I support Colin Simpson in his protest against the use of frogs for a jumping contest. Had I an account with this store, then I would close it at once.

Somebody, sometime, has to take a stand against cruelty to all creatures including frogs, regarded by most people as "just frogs."

Letters, P Smyth. Having seen, on film, a similar contest held in America, with everyone having an uproarious time, to the detriment of the unfortunate frogs, I hoped that this was something that would never become popular in Australia.

But after that, there were plenty of people who saw different sides to the frog issue. These Letters appeared under the heading of *Edible Fred.*

Letters, James Russell. Colin Simpson and other authors of letters to the Editor complaining about the frog-jumping contest being conducted at a leading city store are far too tender-hearted.

I go along with the late Izaak Walton, who advised in "The Compleat Angler": "Thus use your frog... Put your hook, I mean the arming-wire, through his mouth, and out at his gills; and then with a fine needle and silk sew the upper part of his leg, with only one stitch, to the arming-wire of your hook, or tie the frog's leg, above the upper joint to the armed-wire; and, in so doing, use him as though you loved him."

Letters, T Wallace. Those delectable little creatures are not "just frogs," as Alma Kingsmill says most people regard them.

Edible frogs provide a succulent meal for the gourmet - a delight that probably your correspondent has not experienced.

My only fear concerning the frog-jumping contest is that over-exercise may tend to toughen the legs of the competitors - if they are of the table variety.

Letters, Kerwin Maegraith. The ludicrous outburst from Colin Simpson about cruelty to frogs moves one to crocodile tears. Anyone who has had a half-full tank in the country knows the real pleasure frogs get out of a good leap. They have no fear and almost wait for someone to tickle them up for a start. Racing frogs is no more cruel than racing horses or fleas: it is all good entertainment. Certainly nothing to croak about.

But Mr Simpson's silly remark on the radio in "AM," that frog racing might lead to a small boy, engaging in the pastime, eventually becoming a sadist, is a delicious piece of downright nonsense reminiscent of H Bateman, our Australian cartoonist's, immortal cartoon in "Punch," of the tiny lad who breathed on the shop glass window developing subsequently into a habitual criminal. The theory is just as absurd.

Comment. Again, public frog outcry grew too big, and the contest was not re-run next year. Though snail-escaping-a-circle events went on for years.

THE CHURCH AS A CAREER

At the end of August, the *SMH* published its annual careers guide. In this valuable document, it pointed out to youngsters leaving school that there were many jobs they could get, and how to go about landing one. It talked about the major professions,including teaching and nursing. It covered the trades, and various forms of farming. In short, it sought to give coverage to most of the jobs that the babies would want to do.

But one writer found the list wanting.

Letters, Ernest Vines, Presbyterian Church. While I congratulate "The Sydney Morning Herald" on its "Guide to Careers", may I ask why the Christian ministry is apparently omitted, or are ministers of religion meant to be included in social workers?

The guide seems to ignore religion almost completely. Should we not put before all young people the highest purpose - to do God's will and serve God and fellow men?

There was another side to this.

Letters, Sandra Batey. After reading Ernest Vines' letter, I was completely at a loss to comprehend how a past Moderator of the Presbyterian Church could criticise the fact that the ministry was not listed in your "careers" supplement.

To suggest that the ministry is a career to be selected like any other job, for its wages, status and rewards, or even because the applicant is a good public speaker, would horrify Christians everywhere.

I don't think men need to be tempted or lured into the ministry. God is capable of choosing his own ministers without assistance from careers' advisers.

Letters, G Engleheart. Ernest Vines in his reference to "Guide to Careers" is perturbed that theological training is omitted.

He frightens me with his implied anxiety that the young, unless entered in the Christian ministry, will forgo the opportunity to achieve "the highest purpose, to do God's will and serve God and fellow men."

I dare suggest his day will be brightened when he realises that the young by engaging honestly in any of the listed vocations will achieve just that.

Comment. I presume that the first two writers were looking at Protestant churches. The Catholic Church clergy, both priests on the one hand, and brothers and nuns on the other, were different in that they took a vow of chastity for life. How would such an entry read in the requirements for that job? **In addition, candidates must be prepared to abstain from any form of sexual activity for life.** That might be a bit of a turn-off.

Second comment. Still, at the time, recruits from children as young as 13 were accepted, before most of them knew what sex was. Is this **one** reason why 50 years later, there are enquiries and Royal Commissions everywhere discussing the misdeeds of Catholic and other clergy?

THE MASONIC LODGE

A Letter-writer complained that he was excluded from a railway job because he was a Catholic, and not a member of the Masonic Lodge. Apart from the denials that this was true, there were other Letters that showed clearly that the historic hostility between the two groups was still alive and well.

Granted, it had diminished a lot in the last 20 years, but it was apparent that it would take a lot longer than that to be forgotten.

OCTOBER NEWS ITEMS

The Federal Minister for Health reported that **46 children in the last six months were reported as poisoned after swallowing the Pill.** In all cases, this had been an accident when the mother left the pills lying round.

A naked new-born baby was found last night on a rubbish tip in a lane in Melbourne. A man heard its cries, and his wife wrapped it in a blanket and called the police, **It's temperature was 11 degrees below normal when it reached the hospital.** The baby is now doing well. Police are seeking the mother.

Charter flights on airlines will become a **regular** service. The airline must fill all seats on the plane, and can only accept fares if Qantas has refused to provide such a flight....

Fares will be about half of the normal price. Passengers must have a common purpose. It is expected that their usage will be mainly for **groups of people** flying to or from Australia to **visit relatives and friends....**

In practice, **the common purpose did not last for long**. Within a month, the papers were full of adverts for charter flights. **The only common purpose was to get a cheap price.**

The designer of the Sydney Opera House, **Joern Utzon**, was removed from his position last year, before his contract of employment expired. He **has now sued the NSW Government for $349,000** as a consequence.

Twiggy was an skinny beautiful English model who caused a sensation by attending last years' **Melbourne**

Cup in a mini skirt and no hat. This made her famous world-wide even in staid Sweden....

There, four girls started a diet to get down to Twiggy's dimensions. One of them tried so hard that **she collapsed**. She was taken to hospital but caught pneumonia that prevented intravenous feeding, **and she died.**

Recent American tests have shown **links between smoking and lung cancer**. Victoria, as a result, decided to ask cigarette manufacturers to **give details of the tar content of their products**. This was a small step, but it was **the first move by any Australia authority.**

The students of the University of Sydney publish a **weekly paper**. Recently, it included an article that described **how to make LSD from easily obtained chemicals**. The paper was widely criticised in the community at large, and **the Parliament is considering ways to prosecute the paper.**

Three brothers, triplets, at university, **have decided not to register for National Service**. The Minister of Defence says that they must do so, and is ready to throw the book at them. The lads say that they are prepared to **serve in aid organisations anywhere in the developing world, but will not be conscripted to any fighting force**....

Conscientious objectors have been generally despised in all previous wars, but **in such an unpopular war as in Vietnam, it will be interesting** to see how this situation develops. Last year **a conscie**, William White, with much publicity, bucked the conscription mandates. Could these three lads do the same?

VALUE OF DRUNKS

A Letter writer to the *SMH* sent a long and amusing treatise that talked about how valuable the local drunks were to the community. With tongue firmly in cheek, he talked about the work they provided for social workers, hospitals, and police, and extolled them for providing satisfaction to heaps of do-gooders who gave them a handout. The tone of the Letter was friendly, and many a reader would have thought that the drunks bumbling round the streets at night were really welcome visitors and jolly good fellows.

Not everyone agreed.

Letters, Edith Bryant. Perhaps it was in a spirit of whimsy or simulated facetiousness that our correspondent W Henderson has detailed the peculiar doings of his friends who are alcoholics.

Frankly, there is not much cause to be jocular about anything they do, or to find merit for the condition to which they have reduced themselves. Mr Henderson ends his letter with the question: "Please, please, what I want to know is what makes us different from other people?" As a long-suffering member of a family with two alcoholics in its ranks, may I be permitted to supply part of the answer to Mr Henderson's question?

There is a lot of loose, pseudo-scientific talk these days about alcoholism being a disease; of its victims suffering from "personality deficiencies." In good old common language, I have found them selfish and self-centred. Every one of them has started on the road to alcoholism as a social or moderate drinker. Their wounds are self-inflicted and alcohol is the cause of their sickness.

A GOOD RESULT, IN PRIVATE

The Advisory Board of Education is a top government agency in NSW that advises the Minister on matters relating to schools. It has 20 members, drawn from the Department, Parents and Citizens groups, schools, and the community.

At a recent meeting, it considered a recommendation that students sitting for the Leaving Certificate results be each **given a number** so that when results are published, only the student's number will appear and not his name. This, it was said, will protect the privacy of the student, and save him from invidious comparisons with more successful students.

It also said that the names of schools should not be published and that would protect weaker schools also from comparison.

The Board accepted these recommendations and passed them on to the Minister for his approval. Needless to say, this was a departure from a long-established custom, and generated much discussion.

An early writer called the suggested move a most humane and progressive action. He went on to say:

Letters, C Bell. Examination results are of vital importance to the scholar and his or her parents. They **are also a private matter** and surely it is an infringement on this privacy to publish, without the student's consent, complete details of the pass, thus enabling curiosity seekers to hold a field day for comparing the results of the "boy around the corner" with those of the "girl next door" and of the private schools against the State, etc.

The president of the Federation of Parents and Citizens' Association, Mr Bond, was quoted in the "Herald" on September 30 as saying: "The progress of children through school is very closely followed by relatives and friends... they like to see how friends and children of friends have fared... I feel it is a pity to depart from a long-established practice."

Genuine friends and relatives of those concerned would surely be in personal contact, or be in correspondence with them and could, perhaps, be told of a student's number before the results are published. There is little merit in a practice just because it is "long established." Blood-letting was a long-established practice before medics became more enlightened.

Mr Bell, however, did not speak for the majority. One writer wrote that he was so aghast by the suggestion that he was paralysed, but if he was not paralysed, he would write to say how aghast he was.

Letters, Jack Freeman. I wish to protest most strongly against the preposterous suggestion that publication of Higher School Certificate results should be clothed in anonymity, printing numbers instead of names.

This is the inevitable consequence of a pernicious "enlightened" tendency to glorify achievement on the sports field (open to every mediocre intellect) and to regard brilliant academic achievement as something to be ashamed of. There is no surer way of encouraging mental mediocrity. What a future for Australia!

If this move is proceeded with, I suggest that a similar system be employed in reporting Combined High School sports events, so that no school or pupil is made to feel inferior to the top sportsmen.

Letters, P Cotton. Why should the members of the Board be the only ones in a position to compare the academic results of school with school? Surely every interested parent should also have access to this information, as our children are the ones vitally concerned?

Have the members of the Board really become suddenly so solicitous of any possible harmful psychological effects on the students of public comparisons of examination results, or do they perhaps feel that the less the general public knows about the results of this year's certificate the better?

Letters, J Martin. If numbers and not names are published for the Higher School Certificate as has been suggested, it is hardly worthwhile printing them at all, as a jumble of figures will not mean anything to most people, and the students concerned are informed by letter anyway. I am often requested to post the "Herald" overseas and to other States, so that former students may see by the exam lists how their old school friends have fared, and I always look up with interest the exam records of my old school.

For those who have failed I can foresee many embarrassing situations if friends ask them their results. At present if a name is missing from the list the matter is not mentioned.

Some States publish the names and passes in alphabetical order, and this avoids snobbery between schools.

Comment. The Minister ultimately had the good sense not to accept the Board's advice. Other States flirted with the same idea, but none of them adopted the adventurous idea.

A BRAVE SUGGESTION

It is now 22 years since WWII ended, and Australia has gone a long way towards forgetting the Japanese invasion of Australia, and the atrocities that they then committed. For example, there will be a visit this month by the Japanese Prime Minister, Sato, who will be the third Japanese Prime Minister to visit. Trade with Japan has reached record proportions, and Trade Shows in both nations are regular features.

So, *forgetting and forgiving* is gradually working through the community, especially among the Boomers who do not remember the war. Still, this is a long way from the acceptance proposed in the next Letter.

Letters, John Harrison. After the very warm Government-sponsored welcome to Mr Saragat, President of Italy, let us hope that an equally warm welcome is accorded to Mr Sato, Prime Minister of Japan, when he arrives here shortly. After all, Japan is our most important customer, and potentially our most powerful ally in the troubled South-West Pacific.

Japan's rise, literally from "the ashes of war," to become one of the world's leaders in quality, as well as quantity, in such products as ships, radios, cameras, watches, etc., must excite the admiration of even her former enemies. As a new immigration agreement was signed with Italy while Mr Saragat was here, might this not be an excellent time to sign an agreement with Mr Sato for controlled immigration from Japan?

If Italians are suitable as immigrants, why not Japanese? Italy and Japan were both our enemies in the last war. To pretend that Italians are "superior" in some mysterious manner to the Japanese simply because Italians come from Europe is surely quite childish.

Controlled Japanese immigration would greatly benefit Australia in two ways: it would gain us enormous goodwill in Asia, with whom our destiny is increasingly tied, and would gain us the type of brave, clean, tough, extremely industrious citizens our expanding young country needs. The splendid children who have resulted from the intermarriage of Australian Servicemen with Japanese girls show what an asset these people could be. There will never be a more opportune moment than now.

BRISBANE IS STILL ASLEEP?

Gavin Souter, a respected columnist with the *SMH,* had been to Brisbane for his first visit in 15 years. He wrote a piece that said it was still a branch-office town, subservient to Sydney and Melbourne, and getting all their decisions from those sources. He talked about the culture that based so much of its future on the results of the Golden Casket, about the widespread drinking of beer, and its strong trade union mentality. In all, he intimated that Brisbane was a quaint, pleasant, non-industrialised city, with a soporific future.

Letters, P Devine. Gavin Souter's supercilious summing up of Brisbane people's mentality as "Branch-office town mentality", seems presumptuous, since he states that he was in Brisbane "the other day for the first time in 15 years." It savours of the way foreigners fly in to Australia for a week and write a book about Australians.

Brisbane may have been slow to industrialise but if the inhabitants ever become as money-conscious or aggressive as their southern counterparts, it will be their loss. Perhaps some of the less desirable trends of a big industrial city will be avoided by their "procrastination."

Personal Comment. I think most people would agree that Brisbane and Queensland still have much the same image. I do not think this is an accident either. Our Queensland neighbours are, I think, deliberately opting out of much of the rat-race and want a slower pace of life, with more emphasis on their families than on head office.

The constant flow of southerners fleeing the colder climes attests to that. But it is not just the weather, which is better at some times, but hot and sticky and fly-bound in some long seasons. **I think it is the pace of life that is attracting new migrants, and keeping the old hands. Queensland and Brisbane are both here to stay** - and they will stay just as they are. You will not see too many Head Offices in Brisbane.

SOME EARLY THOUGHTS ON ABORTION

All legal jurisdictions in Australia forebade abortions, with different penalties and procedures in place. But times were changing, with women as a class becoming more vocal, and many of them sustaining their efforts by taking the Pill. Two of them, below, were happy to press for reform.

Letters, Beryl Holmes. A recent news item suggested setting up an abortion advice bureau. It would be most beneficial if the woman legally has the final decision.

Certainly any woman in a dilemma would benefit from a full discussion with a counsellor, but ultimately abortions are a matter for individual conscience.

No pressure group should have the right to force a woman to complete a pregnancy she does not want or have a baby she is not prepared to care for.

The number of illegal abortions will decrease only when legal abortions are available.

Letters, (Mrs) Joan Mason. I agree with the Letter from Beryl Holmes, and think the time has come to repeal the NSW law on abortion, which is a hangover from the bad old days when women had no rights. Today we are responsible citizens and each individual should be able to decide for herself whether or not to bear a child.

If the law was repealed and it was left to the patient and doctor like any other operation, there would probably be the same number of abortions than there are at the present time, but without the secrecy and danger.

Certainly, abortion can only be regarded as the cure for failed contraception, but some women can't take the Pill and others prefer not to. We shouldn't be forced to choose between 30 years of pill swallowing or the risk of an illegal operation.

Letters, (Mrs) J Hlavac. The sacredness of human life is a principle which needs to be asserted, and upheld, at all times. Some married women find it "inconvenient" to have a baby at a certain period of their life, and certainly most unmarried girls find it decidedly "inconvenient" to have a baby at all, but **in neither case do they have the moral right to get their unborn babies murdered**.

Suitable foster-parents and adopting parents can be found for legitimate and illegitimate children, through such agencies as the Department of Child Welfare, Catholic Family Welfare Bureau, Church of England Family Service, and others. These agencies can also arrange for pregnant unmarried girls, who cannot remain with their own parents, to be housed in a suitable hostel until the birth of their babies, after which they are assisted with either temporary placement of their babies or else permanent adoption.

There are childless married couples all over the country who are ready and eager to receive and to care for babies. There is no material need, in short, for unborn babies to be murdered. There is no need for a woman to go through life bearing the guilt of the murder of her unborn child upon her conscience.

Letters, J Woolnough. "Happy Mother", in describing the benefits of abortion to her, and Mrs J Hlavac, in describing abortion as murder, summarise the most important arguments for and against abortion.

I would like to comment on the "murder" argument. Our horror of taking human life stems from the all-too-common atrocity of maliciously or callously taking a life in full bloom, a life with a past and a future, and a conscious desire for its own continuance. Strangely enough, we condone even this in case of war or capital punishment, while we quibble over taking a life which is not yet human, not yet conscious and not yet loved.

The extension of our horror of murder to a rigid attitude to taking human life in any circumstances, no matter what the cost in unhappiness to individuals who are very much alive and all too conscious, in contrast to the embryonic state, seems to many of us unreasonable.

Comment. As you can see, many women were quick to point out that abortion involves the taking of a human life. Of course, there were many arguments about when this life becomes sacred, but to these respondents, abortion was murder.

So these women were implacably opposed to any talk of abortion or clinics. **But these were early days,** and it took two decades before these arguments drove people and authorities to **act**.

THOUGHTS ON EATING HABITS

In 2017, there is a much heightened interest in what we eat. We have calorie counts and sugar and fat contents on foods, drinks, lollies, beer, and probably bicycles. If you eat a meat pie, someone will say you will die soon, if you drink full beer, the lite brigade will charge you, if you eat bananas some straight guy will tell you that potash is bad for you. Or maybe that potassium is good for you. It doesn't matter much what it is you eat or drink, there is someone around who can say why three people out of ten have such and such a disease because of this or that, and that you will get fat, or fat feet, or a fatty heart, or thinning hair.

Apart from eating the right foods, there is no shortage of pills, face creams, shiny hair products, and exercise machines to stave off the wicked fat and wrinkles, arthritis, pimples and dull hair. So, this is a great time to eat, drink and be merry.

People back in the 1960's in Australia were not so lucky. A working man then, fool that he was, had bacon and eggs for breakfast, with two sausages and a fried egg and mushrooms. For dinner, a big juicy T-bone steak, with a dollop of mashed potatoes and a helping of boiled cabbage. Of course, everyone hated the cabbage, but even then we all had to have our greens. Then it was followed up with a dessert, maybe a blancmange with ice cream and cream. And a cup or two of tea, perhaps with a buttered slice of Mum's fruitcake. The poor, simple toiler then did not know what was good for him, and that all those Thermal Units were sending him to an early grave.

If only he had known, he could have been having tabouli, lettuce, celery, grated carrot, skimmed milk, barocca, kale, quinoa, acai, and chick peas. What a pity that all you old-timers missed out on all these good things for so long. **If only you had known then.**

Foolish Comment. You can see how devoted I am to the new way of eating. And let me harp on it for a moment. Why is it that, with all the science and wonderful diets and formulae for losing fat, people now in 2017 are 20 per cent bulkier that they were in 1967?

In any case, **back to 1967**. I enclose a couple of Letters that illustrate the eating concerns **then** that were bothering people .

Letters, Judith Pownall. May I support Mrs Faith Fogarty's sentiments and extend them to Sydney cinema-goers who seem to regard their cinemas as little more than a snack bar.

The opening moments of each film, both at the beginning of the performance, and again after the interval, are completely ruined by the crunching of crisp-eaters and lolly-lickers. Any break in the dialogue during the film is instantly taken as a signal to open more crisp bags or unwrap sweets, shattering completely the intense moments of silence often when more dramatic scenes are being portrayed. Indeed, one almost feels compelled to wear earplugs.

What a pity that instead of banning smoking in the cinema, the selling of food in the foyer was not banned.

This second Letter appeared under heading *Vigilantes in the Tuck-shop.*

Letters, E McCormack. Many parents of secondary school students are extremely disturbed by the enormous amounts of confectionery and other unsatisfactory items sold in school tuckshops.

At primary schools, the Department of Education prescribes wholesome food and does not allow the sale of sweets. In the secondary schools, however, the widest choice of edibles is allowed by those who operate the tuckshops or canteens. Very often these powers are misused by committees whose members, while accepting praise for the large profits they make "for the good of the school," justify themselves by saying, "Well the children would buy them anyway, and the school might as well make the profit as the confectionery shop."

Many mothers believe also that school is one place where they and their children should be free from this problem of curtailing the amount of sweets bought by children. The vendors of sweets use all the arts of advertising to flaunt their wares before parents and children.

Surely the Department should set some restrictions on the sale of sweets.

Comment. Note that in the first Letter, the author spoke about "the opening moments **of each film**." This reminds us that in those good old days, when you went to most movie theatres, you got to see **two** movies.

In the first half, a serial and a B-grade movie. Then an interval of ten minutes. After that, there were next-week's trailers and a **Tom and Jerry**, or the like, followed by the feature film.

What a great **Saturday arvo at the** *pichures*.

NOVEMBER NEWS ITEMS

At the moment, **in Britain**, the title and privileges of a peerage are hereditary. That means that **when Lord Muck dies, his heir receives the Title and the right to vote in the House of Lords**. This had been the case for centuries....

The Government will remove these rights, and expects to **cut the number of peers from 1,000 to 300**. New peerages will be created for outstanding persons, but will not be hereditary. Details have yet to be finalised, but the new system will include those principles.

Now here's a bit of **nostalgia** for what are now called rev-heads. **Chrysler will release its new Australian-made Valiant cars and station wagons.** The range will include a six cylinder 160 h.p. model, and a V8 with output boosted to 195 h.p....

When the V8 is sold, it must be fitted with power-assisted front brakes and high-speed nylon tyres **as a safety precaution**.

The Federal Government announced on Thursday that it will provide $68 million to **build dams on the Ord and Emerald Rivers** in the north west of Australia. Farmland around **the region will be irrigated** and the regions are expected to grow traditional crops as well as the **novel crop of cotton**....

On Friday, it said that it will also give $50 million **to build beef roads** in Queensland, Western Australia, and the Northern Territory....

This unexpected generosity surprised the Opposition, and some of them **suggested that the grants were made because a Senate election will be held soon. Such cynicism is, I suspect, not worthy of consideration.**

The ex-Queen of Persia, **Princess Soraya, attended a welcoming function** at the Wentworth Hotel in Sydney. With 400 other guests, she dined on **oysters and beef** and salad. Nothing unusual there, you say....

What was newsworthy **now** was that she accepted twenty debutantes, who all looked as splendid as girls did on such occasions. But, **Ladies, do you remember the ritual of making your debut? What a lot of fun and fuss.** And expense, too....

Remember when **the debutante culture spread from English high society to every suburb in Australia? When girls from Oodnadatta made their debut in the pub at Fink on a Friday night?** Where has all this gaity gone? **Is there a modern day equivalent?**

The popular and **long-awaited film** *A Man for all Seasons* was to be shown at the Vogue Theatre in Sydney's Double Bay. It started off nicely, and the audience was fully engrossed by the manoeuvering of Thomas Moore....

Then all went wrong. There was a change of reel, and **the second reel was in French. This reel went on for 15 minutes.** After that, four later reels were in English....

But too late. Most of the audience got up and left. The manager gave refunds to anyone who asked, but **some of the audience preferred to say rude things.**

TEENY BOPPERS STONED?

The *Sunday Herald* reported that scores of children, some as young as 14 years of age, are attending pep pill parties after school, and have become addicted to a wide range of barbituates, pep-pills and other drugs. Some of them hit themselves with half a dozen powders and pills before classes begin. They sit in class in a drug induced twilight-zone, their minds dazed and senses dulled.

A spokesman for the Drug Foundation said that most of the addicts were girls. "Addiction is often part of the family climate. These kids see their mothers swallowing powders, pep-pills or relaxing tablets."

Letters, G Miller, M Orr, R Goggins. One of the latest pronouncements on the apparent increases in illicit drug-taking and drug-addicition was that of the State Minister for Child Welfare, Mr Bridges, who remarked that he intended to prosecute not only the children, but also parents of any children found to be taking drugs.

He indicated that any parent would be in a position to know when a child was taking drugs because of the child's glazed look and indolent manner. No one for a moment would doubt the need for the Minister's concern in this matter, but indeed such utterances as these create a large doubt as to how much is really known about this problem.

We have also heard that **there is to be formed a Federal Narcotics Bureau,** presumably on the lines of that of the USA, which is to be under the control of a senior Customs officer.

It would indeed be welcome news to learn that personnel of such a body would not be comprised solely of unqualified and unsuited Customs officers - but that some effort would be made to recruit **pharmacists**, who, it is submitted, **are qualified in regard to problems related to drug-taking**.

If the problem is to be approached simply on the same basis as that depicted in a popular TV series, then Australia will, in a very short time, have the same problems as the USA in this matter.

Letters, Pharmacist. It would be desirable, as submitted by your correspondents, Messrs Miller, Orr and Goggins, in their joint letter, to have some qualified persons, such as pharmacists, on any Federal Narcotics Bureau that may be set up.

As a locum pharmacist, I have worked in about 40 pharmacies in NSW. I have found it a sad fact that some of the blame for **the concern over drug-taking can be attributed to certain lawless, unethical members of my profession**. It has been my experience that 10 to 15 per cent of pharmacists make habit-forming and addictable drugs, such as amphetamines and barbiturates, freely available without prescriptions.

Recently the penalty for members of the public found in possession of certain drugs (without a physician's authority) has been made much heavier. There is no doubt that the penalty for pharmacists found guilty of flouting the Poisons Act should also be heavily increased.

Comment. Drugs were a problem that was new to Australia, as you can see from the above information. Clearly, since those days, the supply and the consumption and variety of drugs has multiplied enormously, not just to school children, but to all of the younger ages. Over the years, much intelligent thought has gone into reducing this problem, but it is hard to see that it has yet made a great deal of difference.

Certainly drug busts have made a dent. Customs have learned how to detect and interrupt supplies into the country. Needle exchanges have worked for a few. Education and scare campaigns have had their brief moments. Overall though, **the wastage of the nation's resources in dealing with drugs is still calamitous.**

And it all started with the kids and their pep pills.

UNCLOG THE COURTS

A frequent complaint to the Press was the long delays in having divorce hearings heard. Between the initial filing and the granting of a decision, there was often a period of up to two years, and certainly a wait of one year. This was true for all cases, even undefended actions.

In most cases, the delay was **not** caused by solicitors and barristers accumulating evidence and arguing the finer points of law. It was purely procedural caused by the shortage of staff and judges in the Courts.

Below is a common-sense suggestion that might have helped.

Letters, R Hart. We have read of a number of specious reasons given as to why the mammoth number of cases in the Divorce Court jurisdiction have not yet been heard. None of them is realistic. In fact, if the position were not so serious, it would be laughable.

Many years ago when Mr Andy Lysaght was Attorney-General, it was mooted that there should be night sittings to alleviate congestion in the courts, but the matter was not pursued. Today the position is acute. What is to prevent the appointment now of say, 12 barristers and practising solicitors, well versed in divorce law, to act as Commissioners (as in England) to sit at night empowered to decide cases? They could sit, say, three or four evenings a week in the very same courts as used by the Judges in the day. This could be achieved with a minimum of staff inconvenience.

Comment. This Letter brought forth responses that proposed that schools could be also used **out of hours**, for learning and other purposes. Then that churches would have similar utility. Then cricket fields and sporting fields.

After that, there were tongue-in-cheek suggestions for applying the same strategy to our workforce, with everyone working double shifts, seven days a week. The Editor closed the correspondence after triple-decker buses were added to the list.

WHY MIGRANTS LEAVE

After WWII, this nation thought that we did not have enough population for either defence or for national development, and that we needed to *populate or perish*. One way of fixing this problem was to bring in migrants by the shipload, and most of these came from Britain.

However, by the time we got to 1967, half ship-loads were returning to Britain. Many of these had never intended to remain. They just worked out their bond, had a good holiday, and went back to the misery and doldrums that could then be shared with their old neighbours.

But others, who had come with the genuine intention to stay here, had their own good reasons for leaving, and plenty of advice about what should be done.

Letters, E Dreesde. The Government is perturbed by the reduced inflow of migrants and the increasing trend to return to their homelands. One hears that the prosperity of Western Europe is the reason, but actually this prosperity has declined considerably during the past year and even so the number of migrants remains well below expectation.

People usually migrate or return for economic reasons. **The level of social security is far higher in Western Europe** than in Australia, and one of the greatest stumbling blocks seems to be the means test. It is not so easy for the migrant to compare complicated family allowances, sickness benefits, etc., in various currencies but the means test is easy to understand - and to condemn.

To the migrant it means that if he does well - as he expects to - he will get nothing when he reaches retiring age; only if he fails will he get a pension, and he finds out soon enough how pensioners have to beg and fight to improve their position.

In all West European countries, a Government pension (which sounds better than "old age" pension) is in force and a means test does not exist. A person knows he has a right to his Government pension which gives it a dignity and security which our means test system has not. Moreover, there is a form of adjustment relating to various indexes, thus avoiding the erosion of the value of the pension. Australia spends approximately 6 per cent of the Gross National Product on social security; Italy spends 12 per cent, Germany 14 per cent, the Netherlands 13 per cent, to mention only a few.

To set up a national contributing system is a major task. All other Westernised countries have found the answers to the problems involved. It is a matter of urgency for the Government to establish an Australian scheme.

Social services were **always** quoted as a reason for return. Not just the pension, but also for medical benefits. Britain had a universal health insurance scheme, that provided good basic care for free.

Well, not for free really. It had to be paid for, and the money for these social security benefits came from taxation. So that rates of taxation were higher there than here. No writer mentioned that. Still, the social security argument was a valid one.

There were other reasons given.

One common complaint was that **Australians were not at all refined**, and in many cases, we were decidedly rude. Many writers pointed out in response to this charge that the roughness of Australians was not restricted to the Poms, but was a common feature of life for many Australians. It was part of mateship and important to egalitarianism that no one was special until he proved himself so. They went on to say that the Poms who had the problem had been from privileged classes, and found that here there were no advantages to be had from your schooling, your heritage, your wealth, your clothing or your demeanour. Here, they argued, **it was a classless society. Ruefully, said many a Pom in reply, there was no class at all.**

What about **other** migrants? Take the Italians. Their return rate was much lower. Most commentators said this was because when the Italians came they came as a family, they intended to stay, they saw this as their land of opportunity, and they were determined to take that opportunity. So they worked hard, bought property as soon as they could, and if some of them did not learn the language, they made sure their children did. Ideal migrants, many writers said. Much preferable to whinging Poms.

But another factor was soon to come into play. The White Australia Policy was on its last legs, and there would soon be a trickle of Asians admitted as migrants. Then over the years, it became a swell. It might seem strange that we have never seen laments that Asians have returned to their homes. But it is not at all strange, because few of them do. Maybe, from that one perspective, it could be said that Asians make perfect migrants, preferable to the Poms and dagos.

What do you think?

A personal comment on the British National Health.

Every person in Britain was allocated to a doctor, and most doctors saw their patients as their own flock. It was a bit like Australia in 1950 where a resident town doctor knew his patients and their families, and enquired after their well-being, and was genuinely interested in their health.

An Australian, going to live in a region in Britain, was registered and given a doctor. And he got the free treatment. **But he was not at all part of that doctor's flock.** He was distinctly a black sheep, and was given the off-hand and sometimes rude treatment that black sheep apparently deserve.

If you **do** have the opportunity to go back to 1967, and **do** have the opportunity to be sick anywhere in the world, I suggest that you **do not** go to Britain. You are better off to be sick in sunny Australia.

COSTLY CONVENIENCE

There was a constant stream of Letters to all newspapers decrying the lack of public conveniences everywhere. In the city streets, in tourist locations, at the beaches, at cricket anywhere, on trains, on the highways, and at the opera and theatre. Often, where the facilities were actually there, they were locked up, especially at the weekend when they were most needed. Many times they were dirty, and cleaned only on a weekly basis, Sometimes, they were just plain disgusting. In this latter category, pubs took the cake.

There was another side to this.

Letters, (Mrs) P Carr. I recently had occasion to use the women's toilets on the ferry wharf at Manly. Upon entering with my three-year-old son, I was charged 3c. Later wishing to wash my hands, I could find no sign of either soap or towel. Upon asking I was told by the attendant that no soap was available but if I paid a further 1c a paper towel (midget size) was available. I was flabbergasted!

She then told me that the charge of 3c included 1c for my three-year-old. He did not use the facilities but was too young to leave outside unattended.

I believe this convenience(?) is the responsibility of the Maritime Services Board - what about hepatitis then?

LETTER BOMBS

A Brisbane **woman is in a serious condition after she had both hands blown off by a letter bomb**. She also suffered a fractured jaw and lacerations to her face and body. **One of her children is dangerously ill with a fractured forehead**, and extensive lacerations. Police are investigating.

NEWS AND VIEWS

Letters, Owen Jones, Sec, British Epilepsy Assn.
Recently I had to make inquiries at Australia House in London in connection with the proposed emigration of a sufferer from epilepsy. I was advised **that no person known to be suffering from epilepsy would be permitted into Australia as an immigrant**. The reason for this attitude was given as being "we are building a new country and we only want the best."

This rather indicated that Australia House is under the impression that sufferers from epilepsy are, per se, second-rate citizens, an assumption rather contradicted by such sufferers as Julius Caesar, Dostoievski, Lord Byron, Hector Berlioz, to name but a few. If Australia should be fortunate enough to receive immigrants of this calibre, I can hardly believe that her development would suffer from the fact of their condition. It has always been the task of this Association to disseminate the information that the majority of people with epilepsy are normal, healthy persons with average or above average intelligence, and differing from others only in their tendency to have siezures.

I am shocked to find that the attitude at Australia House should be one of rigid exclusion more suitable to the Middles Ages than to the twentieth century.

Here's some helpful advice from an American.

Letters, Tom Grill. I attended a funeral a few days ago and was shocked at the barbaric way it was conducted. I am an American and I am not saying that Australians should use the methods used in the USA, because the methods used in the States are too costly and meaningless. But, there are some things the Americans do that I feel should be done out here and if not willingly by the people then by order of law.

The funeral procession of about 25 cars was broken by trucks and private cars, which is showing no respect for the dead and the family of the dead.

The undertaker should have enough commonsense and not allow the gravediggers to lower the coffin while the family is standing at the graveside. This, I feel, is cruel and causes a great deal of unnecessary emotional upsets.

The cemetery was a mess and looked more like a tip than a place of final resting (where is the city control?). Not one cemetery in the nation should be allowed to decay to such a state, regardless of its location, be it Canberra or Dubbo. I have seen services for animals carried out better and in a more beautiful cemetery.

The black gloves worn by the coffin bearers are shocking and look more like something worn by a hangman. What's wrong with conventional size gloves in black, grey or white? (The black leather gloves worn at the funeral I attended were about 12-14 inches from the finger tips to the end of the cuff.)

The last few moments of the funeral are remembered for the life of the family and friends - let's make it a dignified remembrance.

Letters, C Madgewick. I'm so sickened by your articles "The Undertakers" that I feel I must protest about the trend disclosed here!

When reading Waugh's "The Loved One" I was so disturbed by the accounts - however sent up - of the American way of death, and knowing that we were sure to be influenced sooner than later, I inserted a clause in my will: I am to be disposed of as cheaply as possible.

Cramped in a coffin, indeed! Who cares? - not I, and I hope my loved ones will have sense enough not to throw good money away.

DECEMBER NEWS ITEMS

Good news for Christmas shoppers. There is a big increase in **forged $10 notes**. Police say this is nothing to specially worry about. It happens every Christmas. But they added, if you **do** get one, **you are stuck with it**. It is a crime to knowingly **pass on** a forged note, and police **left no doubt that they would prosecute offenders**.

The world's **first human heart transplant was successfully done in South Africa**. It involved moving a heart from a young girl to a 55-year-old man.

Yugoslav settlers in Melbourne were celebrating at **their annual ball**. Police were mingling with the 350 guests because, last year, stink bombs were thrown through the windows....

One lad found a fountain pen on the ground. He fiddled with it and, **being a bomb, it exploded** and mutilated his hand, and scared the life out of 349 others....

Police said the bombing was part of **a feud that had carried over from WWII**.

Horse racing in Britain has been banned for an unspecified`time because of an outbreak of **foot-and-mouth disease**.

Senior boys, aged 15 to 18, at **Caufield Grammar School**,will **no longer be required to wear the school cap**. The Headmaster announced this at Speech Night in the Melbourne Town Hall....

He opposed the move, but pointed out that the decision was made by a committee of 20....

He said "Young people need control. There is not enough tradition in schools. **Not the blue jeans and mini-skirted type of freedom they have today.** I believe the boys will want their caps back in a few years...."

It is expected that most Melbourne GPS schools will follow the leader, and that in some, even the straw boater will go. There is no sign as yet of the top girls schools removing their hat-and-gloves formal uniform.

Australia had gone switched to decimal currency last year. Now, select Committees were saying that we should also **move to metric for weights and distance**s. So you **will be able to forget 16 ounces to the pound**, 63,360 inches to the mile....

That might make life a bit easier. Still, **you might have to come to terms with 2.54 cms to the inch**, and one Kg is the same weight as 2.2 pounds....

Comment. Even after all these years of decimal, **I still think of body weight in terms of stones and pounds**, and long distances as being so many miles. A schooner is still 15 ounces....

Yes, I know, I know, I am a dinosaur.

Famous **Australian jockey, George Moore**, had a thrill today. For the first time, **he and his 15-year-old son competed in the same race.** At Randwick racecourse, the father came in third, and the lad finished 12th. **Which goes to show, once again, that the older you get, the better you are.**

TOP HITS FOR 1967

The Last Waltz	Englebert Humperdinck
This is My Song	Petula Clark
Snoopy vs the Red Baron	The Royal Guardsmen
Green Grass of Home	Tom Jones
Penny Lane	The Beatles
Strawberry Fields Forever	The Beatles
Somethin' Stupid	Nancy & Frank Sinatra
Georgy Girl	The Seekers
All You Need Is Love	The Beatles
A Whiter Shade of Pale	Procol Harum
I'm a Believer	The Monkees
Up, Up and Away	The 5th Dimension

MOST POPULAR FILMS IN 1967

The Jungle Book	Phil Harris, Sebastian Cabot
The Graduate	Dustin Hoffman, Anne Bancroft
Eye of the Devil	David Niven, Sharon Tate
Cool Hand Luke	Paul Newman, George Kennedy
Valley of the Dolls	Barbara Parkins, Patty Duke
Bonnie and Clyde	Warren Beatty, Faye Dunaway
Only Live Twice	Sean Connery, Akiko Wakabayashi
The Dirty Dozen	Lee Marvin, Ernest Borgnine
Casino Royale	David Niven, Peter Sellers

BEST ACTOR   Paul Scofield (All Seasons)

BEST ACTRESS   Elizabeth Taylor (Virginia Wolf)

BEST PICTURE   A Man for All Seasons

POPULATE OR PERISH

The above slogan was used over and over by the many vested interests who wanted Australia to bring in lots of migrants to our fine nation. But was there any substance to it? One writer thought not.

Letters, M A Wheeler. There seems to be a widely accepted belief in Australia that since our Asian neighbours are so much more populous than we are, any defence of Australia is impossible. We should examine this assumption.

At one point during World War II, when there was danger of invasion, Australia had one person in uniform for every six of total population. Given our population today of no more than 12 million, this emergency mobilisation would give us two million people in our Armed Services.

To mount even a one-for-one invasion, any enemy would require an army bigger than any expeditionary force the world has ever know. For example, the D-Day invasion plus back-up troops numbered 655,812! If we multiply our two million by the accepted rule-of-thumb of a three-to-one preponderance as the requirement for a successful invasion, we begin to see how unlikely any nation is to attempt this type of foray.

But, add to this again the need to transport this force over hundreds of miles (or thousands depending on who we choose to believe will invade us), and we have a military movement never considered by even the most aggressive of would-be conquerors.

Paranoid personalities, aggressive "isms," world plans of conquest, coloured perils, etc., all considered, it would be interesting to see if the we-are-too-small advocates can produce a nation or group of nations sufficiently interested in the driest continent in the world to want to create all these military records.

KING SIZED FAGS

Any reader who was a smoker at the time will remember the ballyhoo that the tobacco companies promoted as they introduced their new King Sized cigarettes. These were about an inch longer that the previous gaspers, and somewhat fuller, and of course, had new improved filters, and pretty girls in Press photos.

There were a few murmurings in Australia about possible links to lung diseases, so the companies also assured us that the filters **did** filter out any undesirable gasses, and there was also an emphasis on how beneficial they were for the throat. And boy, were they smooth.

Letters, A D'Ombrain. I understand that king-sized cigarettes are to be made even larger now, and I believe the firm marketing them is claiming to be the first to put "king-sized" cigarettes on the market in Australia.

I left off smoking many years ago before these so-called king-sized cigarettes that we see now were on the market, but years before that when I was a youngster I can remember my father having a brand of cigarette called "King Whip" which would put the present-day fag to shame for size. These really were monsters - from memory about five or six inches long - and I can remember smoking them myself later.

Comment. Overseas in the US and Britain there was a growing number of health officials who were saying that there was a link from cigarettes to cancer. This was pooh pahed by most smokers in Australia for years, so we went blithely on puffing and coughing for a long time. Australians never were early adopters of novel ideas and gadgets, and often this has been to our advantage. In this case, though, it cost us dearly.

SUMMING UP VIETNAM

Throughout this book, I have deliberately kept mention of the Vietnam war to a minimum. That was not because it was not important to Australians. It was because it was so important that if I had reported fully on it, all my pages would have been full of war news and its impact.

Now, however, in closing out this book, I must also close out the war **for the year**. I start with a single Letter from each of the pro- and the anti-war views, and they give a fair picture of what both sides are currently saying.

Letters, Will Lewis. I am concerned about the theory of world conquest advanced by Lin Piao when he predicts the overwhelming of the free world by Communism (speech, August, 1963).

I am concerned by the thoughts of the Barton, Thomas and Seidler group that Communism remains a mild form of socialism and that Vietnam is a dirty war. They aren't in a position to give an opinion. Ask a returned airman from World War II, a veteran from Korea or a returned conscript from Vietnam - they would give the right answer.

I am concerned at the rape of Tibet, the massacre of Hungarian students by the Russian tanks in 1956, the near takeover of Indonesia (saved by a miracle) and I'm concerned what will happen to Malaysia and Singapore if we withdraw from Vietnam and allow the Communist "mincing machine" to go through. I am concerned at the evasive, side-stepping speeches of Mr Whitlam - he should be playing Rugby League, not politics. I am concerned at unity tickets - Communist and Labor candidates bracketed together.

I am concerned at a photo in the "Herald" recently of Mr Gallagher and Mr Hill, Australian Communist Party, being welcomed by Chou En-lai and Mao Tse-tung. I am concerned at **700 scientists signing a petition condemning the Vietnam war**.

I am concerned at professors in our universities expounding Marxist theories, and thus turning once Christian students into atheists. There is more evidence of the Resurrection than of anything the Communists can put forward.

I am concerned at the "over mothering" of some of our youth, but again so proud of the real Australian youth who are in Vietnam fighting for what they know is right. They are magnificent, and we should all be cheering them and thanking God they are there.

I am concerned that so many Australians have been brainwashed into believing that America is imposing her policies on everyone else. Remember, America laid her authority very lightly upon a prostrate world at the end of World War II and has had nothing but abuse and contempt since.

So - I'm concerned, and trust that lots of my friends are also concerned.

Letters, Nigel Conrad. I too am concerned. I could pick out the arguments by Mr Lewis and demolish them one by one. I won't bore you by doing that. I will just take one of them, the so-called atrocities of the Reds over the years. I would just point out that America has a worse record. What about Japan in 1840, China a century later, and Mexico and Hawaii, and dozens of other adventures and wars. The nation is bellicose, and loves to stimulate its spending on arms and the killing of its own men and the men of others to promote it arms trades. Always, of course, on someone else's territory.

What I am concerned about is that our men are being killed for no reason. If the French would really get out of Vietnam and give them freedom from colonialism, there would be no agitation, and the country would soon be free of the Reds. But no, we have to send our men to be killed there, not because of any threat to the world, but because paranoid America wants to show the world, by war, how much she loves peace.

My concern is that our men are being killed, and by the look of it, they will continue to be killed in increasing numbers, for years. And for what?

Everywhere you conversed in this nation on every day, reference was always made to the war. The supporters wanted to propagandise, the opponents wanted to convince you that all war was wrong, and that **this war** was wrong and futile and pointless. Both sides said that the other side was heartless, stupid, purely mercenary, short-sighted, and villainous. The pro-war camp pointed to the likely loss of freedom, of all the vulnerable land mass down to Tasmania, the supposed tyranny of Communism. The anti-war group talked about the needless loss of human life, the killing of helpless women and children, the perfidy of the Americans, and the danger to our own kith and kin.

Personal comment. Was there any point to this debate? Not much, I say in retrospect. All debates ended with no change in opinion or attitude, so-called facts tumbled out and were ignored, and life-long friendships were permanently broken.

So, in my view, the debate served only one purpose and that was an important one. **It gave ordinary people a chance to say what they thought.** People, from the cities to Oodnadata, had strong emotions about the war, and there was nothing material that they could **do** about it. **Nothing at all.** They could, of course, and they did, join demos, and write Letters, and plague politicians, but the minds of our leaders were made up. We would go all the way with LBJ, **and that was that**, so all the protests were wasted.

The debates, though, were not all wasted. They at least gave the citizenry a chance to express their feelings. It was better than bottling them up, a gnawing, ever-growing mess of resentment, anger and frustration. They could get some relief by telling the bad guys what they thought of them. Never mind that the opposition was shouting back at the same time, and that no one ever heard a syllable or thought about an argument. It was good to get it off your chest, and to tell the other bugger a thing or two.

But changes in attitude did occur across 1967. It was not the debates that changed them. It was the cold hard facts. It was the slow, gradual, realisation of the brutality of the war, and the fact that our American friends were just as capable of brutality as the Reds, that changed some opinions. And it was a fact that this war would go on and on, and that battle lines would go back and forth, like they did in Korea, and that the big victory today would be forgotten tomorrow.

And it was a fact that the people of Vietnam were losing their lives and their villages to people who were prepared to kill them, as **collateral damage**. What was the point to this war if it was set to go on and on, and the only result was the destruction of the native population?

It was these facts that slowly became apparent. They changed public opinion of the war. **Let me make up some figures** that demonstrate the point. If, at the start of the year, public support for the war was 55 per cent, by the end of the war, I judge it to be 45 per cent. You might say, and you would be right, that it was not really a big swing. But **it did go on at the same rate over the next few years**, and by then the war was most unpopular.

Still, **we fought on until the Americans withdrew from Vietnam in 1973**, with their tails between our legs.

Another comment. I **warned** at the start of this book that **I might offend some readers** here and there. In the last few pages, **in discussing what was one of the hottest issues in Australian history**, I imagine that I might have **regrettably** done exactly that.

The advice that I gave with my earlier **warning** was basically to shrug your shoulders and ignore me. In this case, by now, it will be too late to do this, but you still have the option to say "**silly old bugger and then read on**". If I have offended you, I hope that is just what you will do.

SUMMING UP 1967

Suppose we can do the impossible. Suppose we can say that there was no war in Vietnam and that we had no problems from that source. What was life like here in 1967?

The answer would have to be that it was pretty good. In this nation, **we never think about survival**. We do not have devastating hunger or famine, riots by blacks, revolutions by nationalists, like other nations. We do not even have really bad winters as in other countries. So we don't think in terms of bare survival. **We think in terms of economics.**

Our economy was about as good as you could get. Plenty of jobs, lots of new houses, a few new roads, second cars for the rich, but back-yard barbies under the Hills Hoist for the so-called poor. Life was pleasant with enough petty grumbles to keep most people happy.

Granted there was a glut of ankle-biters and teenagers, and that meant that conversations were banal. Granted that our roads, public transport, pubs, and housing were still miles behind other nations. But we could buy glossy American magazines talking about those things, enough to make our mouths water. And we could watch tons of American movies, listen to their so-called music, and borrow their jeans and caps, and wonder about becoming an American State. But all of these were minor and transient.

More important, most of us were healthy, with a roof over our heads, and warm beds to sleep in, and jobs to keep the money flowing in, and social-services blankets for the unfortunates, and were secure and free. We were better off than most other nations in the world, and most of us secretly knew it, even though we never talked about our luck.

We could grab a beer, or sip some tea, have a sausage sandwich or a cultured lettuce and curried-egg double-decker, and talk about kids, strikes, cars, footie, price rises, other people, and all the insignificant matters that prosperous, contented nations can afford to talk about.

But, sadly, back to reality. Vietnam was impossible to ignore, and that cast a shadow over all the nation. So all I can say is that 1967 was one of the many, many happy and prosperous years that we have had since WWII, **but....**

READERS' COMMENTS

Tom Lynch, Speers Point. Some history writers make the mistake of trying to boost their authority by including graphs and charts all over the place. You on the other hand get a much better effect by saying things like "he made a pile". Or "every one worked hours longer than they should have, and felt like death warmed up at the end of the shift." I have seen other writers waste two pages of statistics painting the same picture as you did in a few words.

Barry Marr, Adelaide You know that I am being facetious when I say that I wish the war had gone on for years longer so that you would have written more books about it.

Edna College, Auburn. A few times I stopped and sobbed as you brought memories of the postman delivering letters, and the dread that ordinary people felt as he neared. How you captured those feelings yet kept your coverage from becoming maudlin or bogged down is a wonder to me.

Betty Kelly, Wagga Wagga. Every time you seem to be getting serious, you throw in a phrase or memory that lightens up the mood. In particular, in the war when you were describing the terrible carnage of Russian troops, you ended with a ten-line description of how aggrieved you felt and ended it with "apart from that, things are pretty good here". For me, it turned the unbearable into the bearable, and I went from feeling morbid and angry back to a normal human being.

Alan Davey, Brisbane. I particularly liked the light-hearted way you described the scenes at the airports as American, and British, high-flying entertainers flew in. I had always seen the crowd behaviour as disgraceful, but your light-hearted description of it made me realise it was in fact harmless and just good fun.

In 1957, Britain's Red Dean said Chinese Reds were OK. America avoided balance-of-payments problems by sending entertainers here. Sydney's Opera House will use lotteries to raise funds. The Russians launched Sputnik and a dog got a free ride. A bodkin crisis shook the nation.

In 1958, the Christian Brothers bought a pub and raffled it; some clergy thought that Christ would not be pleased. Circuses were losing animals at a great rate. The Queen Mother wasn't given a sun shade; it didn't worry the lined-up school children, they just fainted as normal. School milk was hot news, bread home deliveries were under fire. The RSPCA was killing dogs in a gas chamber. A tribe pointed the bone at Albert Namatjira; he died soon after.

✶✶✶✶✶✶✶✶✶✶✶✶✶

Chrissi and birthday books for Mum and Dad and Aunt and Uncle and cousins and family and friends and work and everyone else.

Don't forget a good read and chuckle for yourself.

In 1959, Billy Graham called us to God. Perverts are becoming gay. The Kingsgrove Slasher was getting blanket press coverage. Tea, not coffee, was still the housewife's friend. Clergy were betting against the opening of TABs. Errol, a Tasmanian devil, died. So too did Jack Davey. There are three ways to kill a snake. Aromarama is coming to your cinema.

In 1967, postcodes were introduced, and you could pay your debts with a new five-dollar note. You could talk-back on radio, about a brand new ABS show called "This Day Tonight." There was no point in talking any more to the Privy Council of the Brits – Oz was the only appealing place left to go. Getting a job was easy with unemployment at 1.8 % – better that the 5% 50 years later. Arthur Calwell left at last. Whitlam took his place. Harold Holt drowned, and Menzies wrote his first book in retirement.

****

There are 35 Titles in this Series.

It starts at 1939 and extends for 35 years until 1973.

More details from boombooks.biz

Born in 1968?
What else happened?
AUSTRALIAN SOCIAL HISTORY

RON WILLIAMS

In 1968, Sydney had its teeth fluoridated, its sobriety tested for alcohol with breathalisers, and its first Kentucky Fried. There was still much opposition to conscription to the Vietnam War and demos were everywhere all the time. The casino in Tasmania was approved. We won a pot of gold at the Olympics, Lionel Rose won well, and poet Dorothea Mackellar died at the age of 82.

****

These 35 soft cover books, and nine hard cover, are available from the one-stop shop at boombooks.biz

Soft covers: Yearly from 1939 to 1973

Hard covers: 1939, 1949, 1959, 1969
And for: 1940, 1950, 1960, 1970, and 1958

****